What's Worth Learning?

What's Worth Learning?

Marion Brady

Information Age Publishing, Inc.
Charlotte, North Carolina • www.infoagepub.com

Library of Congress Cataloging-in-Publication Data

Brady, Marion, 1927-
    What's worth learning? / Marion Brady.
        p. cm.
    Includes bibliographical references.
    ISBN 978-1-61735-194-5 (paperback) — ISBN 978-1-61735-195-2 (hardcover) —
ISBN 978-1-61735-196-9 (e-book)
    1. Teaching. 2. Education—Curricula—United States. 3. Curriculum
planning—United States. 4. Thought and thinking—Study and teaching. 5.
Learning, Psychology of. I. Title.
    LB1027.3.B72 2010
    374'.000973—dc22

                                                            2010041404

I'm deeply indebted to the thousands of students in my classes, dialog with whom taught me most of what's in the following pages, and to my brother, Howard, whose arguments constantly forced me to defend and clarify my ideas.

CONTENTS

INTRODUCTION

American education isn't up to the challenge. The evidence is inescapable. Millions of kids walk away from school long before they're scheduled to graduate. Millions more stay but disengage. Half of those entering the teaching profession soon abandon it. Administrators play musical chairs. Barbed wire surrounds many schools, and police patrol hallways. School bond levies usually fail. Superficial fads—old ideas resurrected with new names—come and go with depressing regularity. Think tanks crank out millions of words of ignored advice, and foundations spend billions to promote seemingly sound ideas that make little or no difference. About half a trillion dollars a year are invested in education, but most adults remember little and make practical use of even less of what they once learned in thousands of hours of instruction.

Congress and state legislatures bring market forces to bear, certain that the rewards and penalties of competition will work the wonders in education they sometimes work in business, and nothing of consequence happens. Charter schools are formed to promote innovations, but if the merit of those innovations is judged by scores on corporately produced standardized tests, the innovations are inconsequential. Municipal governments take over failing schools or hand them off to corporations, producing results so poor that statistical games must usually be played to justify contract renewals. Stringent standards are put in place, and tests keyed to them are so high-stakes that failure may shut down whole schools, end teaching careers, and permanently affect the life chances of the young. But performance stays flat.

What's Worth Learning?
pp. ix–xiv
Copyright © 2011 by Information Age Publishing

Cut through the hype and the ideology-driven political rhetoric and it's clear that, decade after decade, institutional performance nationwide changes little. Even schools considered models and pointed to with pride—upscale, beautiful, well-staffed, shipping high percentages of their graduates off to the Ivy League—send most students on their ways with talents and abilities unidentified or undeveloped. Few graduate with their natural love of learning enhanced or even intact.

Perhaps most damning of all is the fact that the human need to understand, to know, to make sense of the world, is one of the most powerful of all human drives, but the institutions we've created to meet that deep human need would close their doors if it weren't for mandatory attendance laws, social expectations, and institutional inertia.

The static state of America's schools stems in large part from a failure to understand a process sometimes called "institutionalization" and its implication for what's taught. In educating, the curriculum is where the rubber meets the road. If it's poor, the education will be poor—no matter state or national standards, no matter the level of rigor, no matter the toughness of tests, teacher skill, school size, market forces imposed, length of school day or year, parental support, design or condition of buildings, generosity of budget, sophistication of technology, administrator wisdom, or enthusiasm of students. A school can be no better than its curriculum allows it to be, and the process of institutionalization, neither understood nor addressed, assures that year after year the traditional math-science-social studies-language arts curriculum will become more dysfunctional.

The process of institutionalization occurs in stages, beautifully explored and elaborated by the late Carroll Quigley in his 1961 book, *The Evolution of Civilizations* (Macmillan).

Stage One: A society has challenges—protecting itself from enemies, caring for the sick, obtaining food, maintaining public order. To address the challenges, organizations are formed—armies, hospitals, police forces, schools, and so on—and effective problem-solving policies and procedures are adopted.

Stage Two: Social change gradually alters the nature of the problems the organizations were created to solve—a different kind of enemy threatens, a plague of unknown cause strikes, once-productive soil wears out. As the problems change, the policies and procedures that worked well in Stage One gradually become less appropriate and efficient.

Stage Three: Eventually, the inadequacy of the original problem-solving approaches becomes too obvious to ignore. Fingers of blame are then pointed at those in the problem-solving organization. More rigorous standards are imposed. Supervisory staffs are enlarged. Policy and procedures manuals grow fatter. Penalties for poor performance grow harsher.

Stage Four: Because the basic problem—failure to monitor change and adapt to it—remains unaddressed, the situation becomes more dire. Reacting, authorities tighten procedural screws, then tighten them again. A kind of Catch-22 dynamic takes over, a variation of, "The beatings will continue until morale improves."

Stage Five: The organization disintegrates or becomes irrelevant. The once-effective problem-solving policies and procedures either disappear or become meaningless rituals.

Education in America illustrates the first four stages of the five-stage pattern. In the colonial era, the basic educational challenge and the curriculum aligned beautifully. The task was to maintain the way of life of a society made up mostly of farmers and craftspeople, a challenge met primarily by modeling. The young grew up immersed in the real world, watching and working with family and neighbors, learning when to plant and harvest, what to do for a sick horse, how to milk a cow, make clothes, build structures. Apprenticeships passed along more specialized knowledge and skills.

After the Civil War, the factory system, urbanization, concentrated wealth, and floods of immigrants changed the task of educating. Building and maintaining railroads, banks, factories, and other giant enterprises called for a few thinkers and many doers. To meet the new challenge, a system of mass education was put in place. It didn't serve the small leadership class very well, but the "sit down, shut up, listen to the teacher, remember the answers, stand up and line up when the bell rings" regimen was appropriate for the millions headed for repetitive manual labor. Again, the educational problem and the solution aligned well enough to keep the process of institutionalization in check.

In the 1890s, very few students attended college, but those who did presented a problem. They came from secondary schools where, in total, about 40 different subjects were taught, and college admissions officers didn't know how to compare their academic records. The situation, prominent educators felt, called for standardizing high school instructional programs, and a ten-man committee of school administrators was appointed by the National Education Association to undertake the task. They submitted their report in 1892, and the following year their recommendations began to be adopted across America, locking in the pattern in near-universal use today.

Big mistake. Change is in the nature of things, and in order to survive, societies must adapt. As the 20th century unfolded, America changed. Work became more specialized and complex; international industrial competition increased; corporations grew larger, more impersonal, and less attached to nation states. Jobs requiring physical labor steadily declined in number, consumerism took off, an ever-rising standard of living came to be considered a right, and the Cold War generated a vague, pervasive sense of uneasiness.

America changed, but education in general, and the curriculum in particular, didn't. It needed to explain a radically different world and help the young develop the intellectual equipment to make sense of it, and it failed to do so.

Enter Stage Three, then Four, where we now are. Boredom, passive resistance, truancy, classroom disorder, dropouts, teacher turnover, an explosion of home schooling, an electorate ill-equipped to maintain a democracy, and all the other problems with public education cited in the professional literature and in mainstream media are obvious indicators of institutional failure, of old problem-solving procedures failing to adequately address new realities.

So screws are tightened. Trust in teacher competence and professionalism disappears—their experience, judgment, and firsthand knowledge replaced by ham-handed, top-down, bureaucratic attempts to monitor and control. "Rigor" is in vogue, with a vengeance. Politicians get campaign mileage from slogans—"Standards!" "Accountability!" "No excuses!" School days and years are lengthened, social promotion outlawed, recess and nap times eliminated, Advanced Placement courses installed, then moved to lower grade levels. Educational administrators thought to be tolerant of "the soft bigotry of low expectations," are replaced by mayors, corporate CEOs, lawyers, and retired military officers. Pay-for-performance schemes are put in place. The message: Screws will continue to be tightened until test scores improve.

The fingers of blame point in the wrong direction. American education isn't suffering from a "people problem" but from a system problem—the "core curriculum" put in place in 1893 and still in near-universal use. America's schools and colleges, preoccupied with covering the material in school subjects and courses, have lost sight of the bottom-line reason for educating: helping learners make more sense of experience.

More than twenty years ago, in a book published by the State University of New York Press titled *What's Worth Teaching? Selecting, Organizing, and Integrating Knowledge*, I argued that the general education curriculum was unacceptable—indeed, that the familiar "core curriculum" wasn't really a general education curriculum at all but a random mix of specialized school subjects that ignored the integrated, mutually supportive nature of knowledge. Their content couldn't be made to integrate in an intellectually manageable way, and as a consequence information was being dumped on learners in amounts far beyond their ability to cope. Even those with the highest scores on standardized tests weren't really learning, but were merely storing information in short-term memory long enough to pencil in the "right" ovals.

In the years since the SUNY book was published, I've watched as America has moved from institutionalization's Stage 3 to Stage 4 and 5. Professional educators have been shoved aside, replaced in policymaking positions by leaders of business and industry working through politicians. There's nothing wrong with American education in general or the curriculum in particular, the new leaders believe. Rigor is needed, and the surest way to achieve it, they're certain, is to bring market forces to bear.

I've had a good seat from which to observe the increasing corporatization of American education. I've watched and listened to my own students, worked with teachers under my supervision, visited schools across America and abroad, gathered materials for Knight-Ridder/Tribune newspaper columns, exchanged thousands of e-mails with professionals on all continents representing many different fields, and read a far greater volume of relevant materials via the Internet than was possible twenty years ago.

In the pages that follow, in language as free of educational jargon as I can make them, I'll explore specific problems with the traditional curriculum; identify a simple knowledge organizer that makes school subjects part of single, coherent, mutually supportive structure of knowledge; discuss the curricular implications and ramifications of that organizer; and illustrate it with a comprehensive course of study for adolescents, older students, teachers, aspiring teachers, and home schoolers. What I'm proposing can be put in place without making bureaucratic waves and ballooning budgets. Indeed, the curriculum has enormous potential for simultaneously vastly improving the quality of general education and radically reducing its cost.

In clear, direct, jargon-free language, Part One of *What's Worth Learning?* identifies more than a dozen very specific problems with the general education curriculum in use in America's schools, colleges, and universities.

Part Two offers a simple solution to those problems—a solution based on the system for organizing information and making sense of it that all humans, even the very young, routinely but unconsciously use. The system isn't an alternative to the academic disciplines and school subjects; it is instead the larger knowledge-organizing system of which the disciplines and subjects are parts.

Part Three explores the implications for and applicability of that system to the familiar subjects and courses presently organizing the general education curriculum.

In Part Four, I describe some of the strategies I've used to help learners from elementary, secondary, and university levels of schooling understand and make formal, practical use of the sense-making system described in Part Two.

The Appendix illustrates and elaborates that system, using "hands on" activities involving familiar, everyday experience that lead learners to construct, for themselves, a logical, practical, comprehensive, coherent, systemically integrated, easily understood and used "master" organizer of knowledge.

PART ONE

PROBLEMS

Spring Road Estates. Whispering Hill Houses. Heslop Homes. Brook-wood Manor. Levitt Park ...

In the years following World War II, the modern subdivision was invented. Bulldozers leveled hundreds of thousands of acres, and crews moved in to mass-produce new houses for millions of Americans. Return-ing military veterans acquired government-guaranteed loans and bought homes in the subdivisions. They were joined by apartment dwellers from the cities who had always wanted "a little place of their own." Other neighbors came as part of a general exodus from rural areas.

As a cultural phenomenon, the subdivision was significant. Locations chosen for tract housing frequently created a variety of stresses on local tax structures. Narrow price ranges populated housing developments with families of similar income, social class, and age. Truck farms that had once been sources of fresh produce were often taken over as building sites. Construction costs dictated street and sewer layouts, determined the physical relationship of houses, and thereby structured to a degree the interactions of inhabitants. Cost considerations shaped the houses them-selves in ways that subtly programmed certain kinds of family life and neighboring. Commercial areas changed location, and older neighbor-hoods changed character in response to subdivision growth.

The social, political, and economic effects of the suburbanization movement in America during the third quarter of the twentieth century were nothing less than revolutionary. No one can understand where

What's Worth Learning?
pp. 1–14
Copyright © 2011 by Information Age Publishing

America has been the last several decades, where it now is, or where it is likely to go without understanding this vast movement.

Where does one acquire the complex of concepts essential to the exploration of this revolution?

Not in the traditional curriculum.

To Americans, individualism is a very positive word. It's often combined with rugged. Rugged individualists, it's believed, conquered the frontier, established the nation, put it on a solid philosophical footing, organized the Industrial Revolution, made American business preeminent, gave the United States a technological edge, established it as a world power, saw the nation through difficult times, and, if given free rein by those in power, will do so again. Most of America's heroes have been perceived as rugged individualists.

This emphasis on individualism obscures the fact that most personal needs are met, most problems are solved, most public goals are attained by organized, collective action. Organizations acquire and wield power, produce goods, and direct social change. Organizations manage the economy, protect life and property, and cushion the cost of accidents and illness. Organizations structure religious worship, design recreation, produce the messages the media transmit, and direct the education of the young. Security, stability, a sense of worth and accomplishment, and assurance that others care—even these kinds of deep psychological needs are met primarily by organizations.

The quality of our lives is largely determined by the quality of the political, economic, social, and religious organizations that structure them. One would suppose, then, that expanding our understanding of human organizations would be a major objective of general education. Surely it's important to understand why and how organizations appear and the variety of forms they take. It would certainly seem important that we understand why some organizations are productive and others aren't, why so few are self-renewing, and how all can be made more responsive to human need. It would seem important that we learn why some organizations function with a minimum of internal friction, but others are continuously wracked by conflict and dissension.

Where does one acquire the concepts essential to an understanding of these entities that play so large a role in our security and happiness?

Not in the traditional curriculum.

In 1947, the Board of Directors of the Bulletin of the Atomic Scientists at the University of Chicago adopted a graphic device designed to heighten awareness of potential catastrophe—the "Doomsday Clock." The design appears on every cover of their journal, with the hands positioned a little before midnight, the number of minutes reflecting what the Board considers the current level of threat to be. Originally, that threat was assumed to come primarily from global nuclear war, but now climate change and new developments in the life sciences are considered capable of doing similar irrevocable harm to humankind.

The nuclear threat hasn't, however, gone away. There are many thousands of bombs scattered around the earth, more are probably being built, and the intentional or accidental explosion of one of them could very well set in motion a fear-driven chain of actions that could escalate out of control.

If that should happen, there will be much that all parties ought to have known. The single most important insight, however, will have had to do with how the mind works in tense and threatening situations. In any unstable relationship, defensive action seems reasonable, even essential, and across the earth there are innumerable unstable relationships—between nations, ethnic groups, social classes, tribes, neighbors, family members, and others. For nations faced, as they often are, with those thought to be hostile, what could be more logical than raising fortifications, building powerful weapons, using strong words to warn of one's ability to prevail in the event of conflict? So defensive actions are undertaken—forts are built or strengthened, weapon stockpiles increased, words sharpened.

Then enemies look across, see the activity, and feel compelled to improve their defensive capabilities. So up go their fortifications and weapon stockpiles, and sharpness of words. In such situations, one's own activity is always considered defensive, and the enemy's activity is always considered offensive. Given each side's assumptions, there's no place to stop the cycle of move and countermove. Each step up makes the next step appear more necessary, more reasonable.

The consequences of the tendency to interpret defensive actions as offensive actions are everywhere apparent. In the U.S., the Middle East, Latin America, Africa, and Asia, defensive actions are being read as offensive actions demanding defensive responses. Closer to home, the same process leads to domestic strife, labor–management conflict, gang violence, neighborhood tensions, family disorganization, divorce, waste, destruction, death.

The costs of not understanding the process of polarization are incalculable. Where will one find an attempt being made to teach the complex of concepts central to an understanding of that process?

Not in the traditional curriculum.

There's nothing particularly complicated or esoteric about suburbanization, organizational dynamics, or polarization. They're the stuff of everyday life, and hundreds of similar summaries could be written. After every summary, the same question could be asked: Where can a comprehensive understanding of the complex of concepts central to understanding be gained? And an accurate response would be: Not in the traditional curriculum.

What can be learned from the traditional curriculum? Much, of course, of unquestionable value. It would be hard to bring the young together daily, put them in the company of reasonably concerned adults, provide them with space and a variety of equipment, and not generate experiences that were educationally defensible. Despite the demonstrable inadequacies of our educational system, most students do learn to read, learn to write well enough to get by, and learn enough math to avoid being cheated at the checkout counter. And at least some students realize much of their potential—learn to speak a foreign language, solve difficult intellectual problems, create beautiful forms, work effectively with others, find satisfaction in an understanding of this era and the place they occupy in it, and maintain reasonable control over their own fates. Notwithstanding the mainstream media's routine use of scores on international tests to make America's schools look as sorry as possible, a fair reading of the statistics sends a different message. Indeed, as mountains of research indicate, the main problem isn't incompetent or lazy teachers, union foot dragging, sub-standard colleges of education, "the soft bigotry of low expectations," inadequate funding, failure to employ market forces, lack of technology, or some other frequently cited reason for poor school performance, but the high level of childhood poverty. If students suffering from poverty and poverty-related factors are removed from the statistics, American schools come off very well compared to the best schools elsewhere.

SPECIFIC CURRICULAR PROBLEMS

Schooling in America produces successes, but the general education curriculum doesn't deserve much credit. What's taught—the actual content of the lectures, books, instructional units, films, videos, subjects, courses, programs, and all the rest—isn't a product of a comprehensive, rational theory or plan. It's not a systematic sampling of humankind's accumulated knowledge. It's not the result of a thorough, current analysis of the needs of individuals or the larger society. It's not a grand design worked out by our best minds. Incredible as it may seem, American education, this vast institution that consumes so much of our wealth, time, and energy, offers the young not a coherent, logically organized structure of knowledge but a random heap fashioned by ancient concerns and assumptions, political expedience, accident, intellectual fads, hysteria, special interests, and myriad superficial views of the purpose of educating.

As I noted in the Introduction, the so-called "core curriculum"—the familiar mix of math, science, language arts, and social studies disciplines now in near-universal use in America's schools—was recommended by the Committee of Ten, appointed by the National Education Association. The Committee didn't discuss the organization of knowledge, didn't talk about learning theory, didn't reflect on the needs of the Republic, didn't speculate about the trends of the era, didn't warn of the dangers of adopting a static curriculum in periods of rapid social change. Those and other matters relevant to what schools should teach never came up. Primarily concerned with simplifying the selection process for college admissions officers by standardizing the transcripts of the tiny percentage of students then graduating from high school, the ten met for three days in Saratoga, New York in the fall of 1892, made their recommendations, and the following year the curriculum that still shapes education in America and much of the rest of the world was adopted. Multi-layered bureaucracies quickly froze the committee's work in rigid place.

The curriculum now in near-universal use in America's classrooms was poor when it was adopted, and has become more dysfunctional with each passing year. About the only thing it has going for it is familiarity and the comforts of ritual. It's accepted not because it's good, but because, like most rituals, it's unexamined. Its problems are myriad and serious.

Problem: The Traditional Curriculum has no Agreed-Upon, Overarching Aim

At an operational level, the obvious aim of most educational institutions is to "cover the material." The question that wasn't on the agenda of the meeting in Saratoga, and that's not yet been seriously examined is, "Why? What's the point? What's the bottom-line aim of schooling?" Is it to teach the core disciplines? Keep the US economically competitive? Prepare the young for democratic citizenship? Instill a love of learning? Sharpen problem-solving skills? Explore key concepts? Teach "the basics?" Raise standardized test scores? Learn to work well with others? Improve thinking skills? Prepare students for useful work? Explore the "eternal questions"? Create informed consumers? Develop character? Transmit societal values? Instill virtue? Respond to student needs? Foster creativity? Expand self-understanding? Solve social problems? Promote love of country? Exceed world-class education standards? Build self-esteem? Explore broad themes? Something else?

Most of those aims, all gleaned from educational literature, have merit, and a good curriculum will accommodate many of them. But every one of them, if seriously pursued, would require the use of particular instructional materials, particular teaching methods, particular tests, even, possibly, particular physical facilities and equipment. It's no more possible to pursue more than one overarching aim effectively than it is to set out on a journey and arrive at two different destinations at the same time.

The present situation is acceptable only because it's taken for granted. What's taught isn't taught because it's seen as moving individuals or the larger society toward some greater good, but because it's what was taught last year. And what was taught last year was taught because it was taught the year before that.

Problem: The Traditional Curriculum Disregards the Brain's Need for Order and Organization

The human brain stores and processes information using an elaborate category system, rather like a mental filing cabinet. The cabinet has drawers, and in the drawers are files, sub-files, sub-sub-files, and so on. "Environment" is a big drawer, "climate" is a file within that drawer, "cloud cover" is a sub-file, "cumulus" is a sub-sub-file, and so on.

In order to make sense and be remembered, new ideas have to fit within this elaborate filing system.

```
ORGANISM
      PLANT
            TREE
                  CHESTNUT
                        AMERICAN
VEHICLE
      MOTOR
            AUTOMOBILE
                  FORD
                        TAURUS
                              2009
```

At each level within sequences like these there are more entries at the same level of generality. The levels, their sub-entries, and the relationships between levels and between entries are, collectively, a "conceptual structure." To "understand" a category means to be familiar with its levels, entries, and relationships. To "grow in understanding" means to discover new categories, new entries within the categories, and new relationships between them.

It sounds complicated, but little kids manage it quickly and easily. To a toddler, every four-legged creature may at first be a "doggy." Soon, however, some of those "dogs" become horses, other cows, and still others kittens. Eventually, the label dog is replaced with the broad category animal. New entries are added, and as understanding grows, each of the entries becomes itself a level with its own subsumed entries. Dogs become terriers, French poodles, and spaniels—categories which are in turn elaborated even further. "French poodles" become "standard," "miniature," "toy," and so on.

All humans make constant use of this sophisticated knowledge-organizing system. There's probably no limit to how much information the system can handle, but it presents educators with a challenge. The main reason learners forget most of what they once "learned" in school is that it never made it into the brain's knowledge-organizing system. Instead, it just floated around in the learner's short-term memory until the test was over and a grade assigned.

There's an old pedagogical theory: "If you throw enough mud on the wall, some of it is bound to stick." It sounds plausible, but it's wrong. Instruction that dumps information that can't be fitted logically into the learner's "master mental filing system" will soon disappear from memory.

Problem: The Traditional Curriculum Fails to Exploit the Teaching Potential of the Real, Everyday World

Much traditional instruction hands learners words about reality—about people, other forms of life, the elements, language, the universe, physical forces, the past—and then makes the words themselves rather than that to which they refer the primary subject matter.

The difference between reality and words about reality is crucial—the difference between listening to music and reading about it; between touching and being told about touch; between, finally, a dynamic and a dead curriculum. The teacher who says, "How does it feel to be afraid?" is probing reality. The teacher who says, "What's the author saying about how it feels to be afraid?" is, more often than not, checking the student's memory of words on a page.

The traditional curriculum—keyed not to reality but to what those thought to be experts say about reality—makes education primarily a game played with textbooks, teacher talk, and tests. The winner isn't the most thoughtful or perceptive kid, but the one with the best memory. The teaching skills required are minimal, mostly those useful for distributing information. It's a task that could be done quicker, easier, and a lot cheaper with machines.

More importantly, the inherent complexity of uninterpreted reality, directly confronted, requires the use of every known thought process, and does so in a perfectly natural way. Pedants, not just comfortable with abstractions but often preoccupied by them, tend to forget that no abstraction comes even close to the real, everyday world in its intellectual challenge.

A curriculum that directs learner attention to the real thing, on the other hand, challenges, stretches abilities, has no finite bounds. It keeps teachers properly humble, makes clear the unavoidable subjectivity of the task, and produces results that lie far beyond our present primitive ability to evaluate.

Real teaching isn't about distributing information, but about figuring out how the "pictures" of the real world learners have in their heads are blurred or out of focus and helping them make them clearer. Most frequently, this isn't done by telling them what some authority believes is "true," but by raising questions that cause the learner to re-examine an idea or assumption. It's a skill that may or may not come with experience, but if it does, it develops slowly, and it can't be taught in schools of education.

Problem: The Traditional Curriculum Lacks Criteria for Determining What New Knowledge to Teach, and What Old Knowledge to Discard to Make Room for the New

If information didn't expand, if new disciplines weren't demanding to be recognized, if the world didn't change, if our ability to deal successfully with critically important problems was routinely exhibited, then an educational machine that pounded out the same familiar fare generation after generation would be acceptable. But the world isn't static; most of what needs to be known isn't in textbooks, and there's no all-wise referee saying that, taking all relevant factors into consideration, the math department should get, say, 12% of the learner's time and the history department should get 9 or 14%. Such issues are settled by tradition, politics, budgets, and other factors, of which logic isn't one.

There's time to teach only the tiniest fraction of all there is to know. That means that decisions have to be made. Wise decisions depend on sound priorities and, because these have never been thought through for the traditional curriculum, special interests tend to step in and promote self-serving priorities. Industry, for example, may demand that schools turn out more mathematicians or scientists not because they're actually needed, but because they know that if there's a surplus, competition will keep salaries low.

Problem: The Traditional Curriculum Ignores Important Fields of Knowledge

It's usually taken for granted that the general education curriculum provides learners with a sort of "knowledge starter kit." Textbook titles sometimes begin with the phrase, "An introduction to…" making it clear that there's more beyond what the book in hand provides. It's also usually taken for granted that the mix of courses in the core curriculum encompasses all important fields of knowledge, and that having "covered" them, the young have a comprehensive foundation upon which to build. They have "the big picture" and are ready for life or pursuit of a specialization.

That's hardly the case. There are fields of study absolutely essential to making sense of ordinary experience that aren't even hinted at in the general education curriculum. One such field is what the anthropologist Edward T. Hall called "proxemics." It has to do with relationships between a person's feelings and actions and the immediate environment.

Consider, for example, a traditional classroom and its furnishings. The typical student desk sends a silent but powerful message about learning: that it's a static process, that the learner is expected to be passive, that what's important is most likely to come from the direction the desk faces. The size of the room, the height of the ceiling, the windows or lack of them, the arrangement of desks, the distances between them, the relative size of the areas "owned" by students and teacher, the color of the walls, the level and quality of the light and sound, the floor covering, whether or not passers-by in the hallway can see in—all these and more affect classroom dynamics, shaping values and attitudes in subtle but important ways.

And what's true in classrooms is true in homes, offices, department stores, and everywhere else. Vast amounts of money have been spent studying shopper behavior in supermarkets in order to maximize purchases. That fact alone should remove any doubt about the importance of understanding the relationship between behavior and environment. Every environment manipulates, which means that failure to understand how it does so limits individual freedom.

There are other fields of study equally essential to the sense-making process that are being ignored by the traditional curriculum, but no mechanisms are in place to even evaluate their merit, much less assign them space in the curriculum.

Problem: The Traditional Curriculum Fails to Capitalize on Human Variability

Education journals, handbooks, course catalogs, promotional brochures, inscriptions over building entrances, statements of vision, aim, and purpose, platform rhetoric, and so on, often claim that an educational institution's policies and programs "respect individual differences," or, "develop the whole person."

The phrases strike a responsive chord because they reflect a core American value. Individualism, initiative, spontaneity, and creativity are viewed positively. We admire the independent thinker, think personal autonomy is a very good thing, and believe every person should be helped to realize her or his full potential.

But we create and continue to maintain an educational system at near-total odds with what we say we believe. Instead, we standardize. Just about every school in the country—public, private, parochial, charter, magnet, virtual, home, whatever—uses the same calendar, the same curriculum, the same or very similar standards, the same nationally distributed, interchangeable textbooks, and the same corporately produced standardized tests. The lack of public protest testifies to the inability of most to realize how at odds are our values and our approach to educating.

Every student, for example, must take higher math, this despite the fact that in any randomly selected school, it's unlikely that more than a small handful will have enough mathematical ability and interest to consider making active, productive use of it. How much sense does it make to put a math whiz in an algebra classroom with 25 or 30 aspiring lawyers, dancers, automatic transmission specialists, social workers, surgeons, artists, hairdressers, language teachers? How much sense does it make to put hundreds of thousands of kids on the street because they can't pass algebra?

What's true in math is true in every field. We argue that introducing the young to all the academic disciplines is necessary to make them "well-rounded," say that it contributes to some vague concept called "mental discipline," believe that population mobility requires a high level of standardization. But these are rationalizations. America's system for educating is in an advanced stage of institutionalization and calcification. Maintaining it, not maximizing individual potential, explains the education game being played.

More Problems, and the Biggest Problem of All

Those six just begin a list of problems with the curricular status quo. As ordinarily implemented, the traditional curriculum also fails to address critically important moral and ethical issues, ignores alternatives to text and speech as sources of learning, vastly overworks short-term memory to the neglect of all other thought processes, and casts learners in unnatural, passive roles. It fragments the profession by discipline, making dialog dif-

ficult and discouraging collegiality, lends itself to superficial methods of
evaluation, neglects the basic processes of creativity and knowledge generation, and is extremely inefficient and unnecessarily costly.

One problem, however, stands above all the rest in seriousness—the
familiar curriculum's failure to model the fundamental nature of knowledge. In the real world, the world an education is supposed to help learners understand, everything relates to everything. It's a systemically-
integrated whole, the parts of which are mutually supportive. The curriculum should model that whole, should help learners discover or create a
corresponding conceptual framework or structure of knowledge, and it
doesn't. Instead, it breaks reality into myriad small pieces and studies
each piece in isolation, with hardly a hint either of how the individual
pieces relate to each other or how they fit together to form the whole.
Consider:

> We want a pair of socks. Those available have been knitted in a Third World
> country. Power to run the knitting machines is supplied by burning fossil
> fuels. Burning fossil fuels contributes to global warming. Global warming
> alters weather patterns. Altered weather patterns trigger environmental
> catastrophes. Environmental catastrophes destroy infrastructure. Money
> spent for infrastructure replacement isn't available for health care. Declines
> in the quality of health care affect mortality rates. Buying socks, then, is a
> matter of life and death.

Making sense of this simple cause–effect sequence while staying within
the bounds of the traditional curriculum is impossible. Understanding
requires not only some grasp of marketing, physics, chemistry, meteorol-
ogy, economics, engineering, psychology, sociology, political science, and
other fields not usually taught in school, but an understanding of how
those fields fit together systemically. The traditional curriculum gives
learners a little biology, a little poetry, a little algebra, a little government,
a little of this and a little of that, but no help at all in meshing them to
form a coherent whole. Indeed, as any school catalog will make clear, the
trend in formal, institutionalized education is in the opposite direction,
away from integration, toward ever-greater specialization. Academic
departments, conferences, scholarly papers, arcane vocabularies, professional journals and other publications, even the physical layouts of many
institutions—all work against knowledge integration.

Failure to build a coherent, integrated sequence of studies reflecting
the holistic nature of knowledge can't be blamed on lack of warnings
about the problem. Scholars have been insisting for centuries that adequate sense can't be made of experience by ignoring its integrated nature.
Even Rene Descartes, that master of slicing reality apart, said in Rule 1 of
his 1628 treatise, *Rules For the Direction of the Mind*, "If, therefore, anyone

wishes to search out the truth of things in serious earnest, he ought not to select one special science; for all the sciences are conjoined with each other and interdependent...."

Herbert Spencer discussed the matter in his 1859 essay, "What Knowledge Is of Most Worth?" Alfred North Whitehead, in his 1916 Presidential Address to the Mathematical Association of England, told educators they needed to "eradicate the fatal disconnection of subjects which kills the vitality of the modern curriculum."

Internationally known Trappist monk Thomas Merton, poet, social activist, student of comparative religions, and author of more than 60 books, in *Contemplation In a World of Action*, wrote, "The world itself is no problem, but we are a problem to ourselves because we are alienated from ourselves, and this alienation is due precisely to an inveterate habit of division by which we break reality into pieces and then wonder why, after we have manipulated the pieces until they fall apart, we find ourselves out of touch with life, with reality, with the world, and most of all with ourselves."

Harlan Cleveland, diplomat, U.S. Assistant Secretary of State for International Organization Affairs, President of the University of Hawaii, and founding dean of the University of Minnesota's Hubert H. Humphrey Institute of Public Affairs, in the July 1985 issue of *Change*, wrote, "It is a well-known scandal that our whole educational system is geared more to categorizing and analyzing patches of knowledge than to threading them together."

John Goodlad, after a massive, multi-year study of American high schools culminating in a 1984 McGraw-Hill book titled, *A Place Called School*, wrote, "The division into subjects and periods encourages a segmented rather than an integrated view of knowledge. Consequently, what students are asked to relate to in schooling becomes increasingly artificial, cut off from the human experiences subject matter is supposed to reflect."

In 1985, from the Association of American Colleges' Project on Redefining the Meaning and Purpose of Baccalaureate Degrees, came a report titled, "Integrity in the College Curriculum, A Report to the Academic Community." In clear, simple language, the framers of the report said, "We do not believe that the road to a coherent education can be constructed from a set of required subjects or academic disciplines."

Peter Senge, scientist, and director of the Center for Organizational Learning at the MIT Sloan School of Management, wrote in his best-selling 1994 book, *The Fifth Discipline*, "From a very early age, we are taught to break apart problems, to fragment the world. This apparently makes complex tasks and subjects more manageable, but we pay a hidden, enormous price. We can no longer see the consequences of our actions; we lose our intrinsic sense of connection to a larger whole."

WHAT'S MISSING AND NEEDED

The conclusion is inescapable. If all knowledge is related, then any curriculum the elements of which aren't related in ways every learner can understand isn't a good curriculum.

The education establishment's usual suggestion for integrating knowledge is interdisciplinarity, but it simply isn't possible to pull together a mix of specialized disciplines and integrate them in a way that's logical and intellectually manageable. There are, of course, a near-infinite number of disciplinary parallels and intersections that can be explored in interesting and useful ways, but randomly combined, such exercises can't be made to form a coherent curriculum. The academic disciplines didn't begin life as parts of a whole, and can't now be directly integrated. Their differing aims, differing vocabularies, differing conceptual frameworks, and differing levels of abstraction see to that. An acceptable general education must pull in and organize everything the learner knows, both "school knowledge" and "street knowledge," and make it all part of a single, logical, sense-making model of reality.

The academic disciplines and the school subjects and courses based on them do a satisfactory job of organizing knowledge about various random parts of reality, but neither singly nor in any combination can they be made to encompass and organize everything learners know. Most of our understanding of complex problems, most of our awareness of relationships in the real world, we pick up from firsthand experience and from the media, from those paying little or no attention to the artificial, arbitrary walls academia has erected around disciplines, subjects, and courses.

The curricular status quo has always been unacceptable, but following World War II, major advances in curriculum design were being made based on General Systems Theory and research into how the brain processes and stores information. That progress ended abruptly in the late 1980s, when leaders of business and industry shoved educators aside and, working through the U.S. Congress, took over education "reform." The "standards and accountability" mandates then imposed on the fifty states resulted in the writing of thousands of subject-matter standards reinforcing the traditional, fragmented curriculum, and the high-stakes, corporately produced standardized tests accompanying them forced educators to teach to those standards or risk losing their jobs and reputations. What the new "reformers" thought was progressive was actually highly reactionary, embedding even more deeply in bureaucracy and in public consciousness a flawed view of the nature of reality and how best to make sense of it. The 1893 curriculum was in large part a product of the industrial era in which it was adopted, when division of labor, standardization of parts, hierarchical management structures, and mass production were revolutionizing American industry.

A metaphor may help clarify the problem. Think of present subjects and courses as pieces of a jigsaw puzzle. Attempting to assemble a puzzle, most people begin by studying the picture on the lid of the box and doing a rough sort based on it. The traditional curriculum has no counterpart to that picture. Its specialized studies have given us much, and many more such studies should be made available to learners, but neither individually nor collectively are they up to the curricular challenge. There's no counterpart to the "big picture," and too many pieces are missing to allow sense to be made.

For general education, what's needed is a single, comprehensive, "supradisciplinary," knowledge-organizing, systemically integrated, stand-alone discipline. In the following pages, such a discipline will be described.

The familiar specialized studies that now make up much of the curriculum need not be discarded. This new discipline pulls all that seemingly random knowledge together to form a coherent, mutually supportive whole, integrates it with the learner's personal experience, makes use of every known thought process, and constantly demonstrates its relevance and everyday practicality. It does all this in a way simple enough to be easily understood and used by adolescents, but complex enough to challenge the most brilliant graduate students. Its efficiency can free up time for courses, programs, projects, and activities that develop the vast and varied abilities and interests learners bring with them to school but often lose as traditional instruction narrows and standardizes options for study.

PART TWO

A SOLUTION

We take for granted the need to organize information. A system of organization—the alphabetizing of names—makes it possible to find, in a matter of seconds, a number in a phone book. A system of organization—the periodic table of the elements—made it possible to predict the existence of the element germanium before it was actually discovered. A system of organization modeled by a chart makes it possible to quickly grasp a company's approach to the distribution of human resources. Systems of organization make it possible to find a particular book in a library, a particular kind of cereal in the supermarket, a particular taillight in a well-run junkyard, a particular departure gate for an airplane flight.

We take our systems of organization for granted, but it's no exaggeration to say that systems of organization make civilization possible. For everything from the most mundane action—from getting a glass from a kitchen cabinet, to the most esoteric research in an obscure field of study—it's awareness of a system of organization that guides effort. The better the system, the clearer the thought and the more efficient and effective the action. From this it follows that if we want to improve something, taking a long, hard look at its system of organization is a good place to start. We want to improve education. We should, then, take a long, hard look at its systems of organization.

There are plenty of them to examine. Systems of organization sort students, assign them teachers, set schedules, lay out instructional programs, check on individual and collective performance, establish consequences

What's Worth Learning?
pp. 15–69

for success and failure—in short, systems of organization control the whole of the educational process from start to finish.

Educators, worried about system effectiveness and almost always under the gun from politicians, policymakers, and the general public, fiddle with these systems, experimenting with different ways of sorting students, different staffing arrangements, different schedules, different evaluation strategies, different procedures for controlling and motivating behavior.

Unfortunately, the one system of organization that gets the least attention is the one that's far and away the most important—the student's mental system for organizing knowledge.

Think of the learner's brain as library, as supermarket, as junkyard. Then, follow the student through the school day, watching and listening as into that library, into that supermarket, into that junkyard, a conveyor feeds a constant stream of information and dumps it in an unorganized heap. That which we see as essential to functioning in every other dimension of daily life—a system of organization—is all but ignored in the one place where it matters most: in the mind of the learner.

Traditional instruction does, of course, make use of information organizers. The curriculum is the main one; the arts, sciences, and humanities are major sub-organizers. Academic disciplines such as biology, sociology, astronomy, chemistry, and so on are sub-sub-organizers. Individual subjects and courses such as human anatomy, urban sociology, and inorganic chemistry are sub-sub-sub-organizers. And topics, themes, concepts, or some other unit of instruction within these sub-sub-sub-organizers generally organize knowledge at yet other levels.

But these organizers, based as they are on the general education curriculum adopted in 1893, are of limited value to learners. They serve as "collection bins" for information, usually in the form of myriad "facts," but the conventional wisdom notwithstanding, isolated facts serve little real-world purpose. The assumption that accumulating and storing them in memory is the learner's main task is an enormous obstacle to meaningful curriculum reform.

Charles Dickens captured that assumption in his 1854 novel, *Hard Times*. He has Schoolmaster Thomas Gradgrind saying, "Now what I want is Facts. Teach the boys and girls nothing but Facts. Facts alone are wanted in life. Plant nothing else, and root out everything else. You can only form the minds of reasoning animals upon Fact; nothing else will ever be of any service to them.... In this life, we want nothing but Facts, sir, nothing but Facts!"

In traditional schooling, facts have a life of their own. They're almost tangible—capable of being "stuffed" into heads, "crammed" in preparation for an exam, or made to "come alive" by a history teacher. They're "cold," "hard," can be "stored," "filed," and "mixed up." Kids who don't have enough of them are "empty headed," while others can have so many, "facts are running out their ears."

It's the ability to recall facts that allows test takers to fill in the blanks on worksheets, and pencil in the proper ovals on the standardized test items. Facts get highlighted and underlined in textbooks, noted in notebooks or typed into laptops as a professor's lecture proceeds. It's knowledge of facts that earns parental praise, and failure to learn them that brings indignation: "My granddaughter is in the eleventh grade, but she can't find Belgium on a map. She didn't even know it was a country."

How do kids learn, really learn—learn in ways so powerful that knowledge is permanently fixed in their minds and ready for a lifetime of use? Is it mostly a matter of listening and reading, then remembering what's been said and read, or is another, less-obvious process at work?

We lay in a crib, and nothing much happened. We made noise, and someone picked us up, changed our diaper and gave us something to eat. We had discovered a *relationship* between noise and reaction. We learned.

We grew and discovered a relationship between the time of day, our father's mood, and the likelihood we'd get a "yes" if we asked to borrow the car. We learned.

We became adults, went into various fields and discovered relationships between urban design and crime rates, between age and susceptibility to advertising, between certain fuel additives and cleanness of fuel burn, between emotions and physical health, between religious belief and reaction to social change, between technology and family instability, between global warming and insurance rates. We learned.

Yes, we learn from lectures. Yes, we learn from reading textbooks. Yes, we learn from running down references and searching the Internet. But most of the insights that guide us through our daily lives don't come from lectures, books, libraries, or the Internet. They come from variations on that early experience of crying and getting attention—discovering relationships between things we didn't previously think were related.

It surely follows, then, that facilitating and enhancing the relationship-discovering, knowledge-*constructing* way we learn should be the primary emphasis of classroom instruction. Rarely, however, is that the case. The usual emphasis is instead on the comparatively minor, passive, knowledge-absorbing, fact-collecting approach. The costs of this misplaced emphasis are far greater than we think. They won't show up on standardized test scores, won't show up on report cards, won't show up in education statistics that politicians are likely to cite to promote their political agendas or ideologies, but they're a major reason why the institution is in crisis, and why that crisis will only deepen if the instructional emphasis doesn't change.

Moving the education establishment, someone has said, is harder than moving a Jell-O elephant. But if the institution is to meet its responsibilities, that challenge must be met. Facing a complex, dangerous, unpredictable future, the young can't rely on the wisdom of the elders. They'll need answers to questions the elders have neither asked nor answered, so will have to generate them for themselves. There is, then, no realistic alternative to making the relationship-exploration process the primary focus of instruction.

Unfortunately, traditional instructional materials for the core curriculum, emphasizing mere student recall of "expert" opinion about patterns and relationships within circumscribed fields, give educators little support. Textbooks and other standard instructional materials simply aren't designed to explore relationships. Standards documents are often prefaced with statements saying the standards identify what students should know and *be able to do*, but the "able to do" part invariably gets the short end of the stick. Because it's easy to test what learners remember, but impossible to test in any machine-scored way what they can actually *do* with what they know, it's the "know" part that gets tested. And, because teachers have little choice but to "teach to the test" if they want to keep their jobs, the autonomy that teachers and learners need if they're to use the real world as their primary "textbook" is missing.

Just as there's no way to know which facts might need to be known, so it is that, given the vast differences in individual learner experiences and situations and the inability to know what the future holds, there's no way to know which patterns and relationships need to be known. For this reason, it's the *process* of relationship exploration that should be of primary concern. Fortunately, for that purpose, instructional resources are readily available, for they're everywhere, and free. All it takes to make use of them are teachers interested in the complexities of the everyday world, respectful of their students' intellectual potential, and able to ask probing questions.

What's the relationship between various arrangements of classroom furniture and discipline problems? Between school design and energy consumption? Between student television-viewing preferences and reading patterns? Between age and crime rates? Between house design and intra-family interaction? Between favorite games and personality traits? Between school size and dropout rate?

Start students with one or two questions like those, and they'll soon be flexing their intellectual muscles, generating their own hypotheses about possible relationships, and extending the horizons of their interests in unexpected directions.

There's an old adage: "Give a man a fish and you feed him for a day. Teach him to fish and you feed him for a lifetime." It has a parallel in education: "Teach learners answers and you prepare them for the next exam. Teach them how to ask question about relationships and you prepare them for life."

TIGHTENING THE INSTRUCTIONAL FOCUS

A major problem with teaching facts is that they're infinite in number, and no criteria are in place to establish their relative importance. Put teachers of all fields of study together in a room and not let them out until they'd reached agreement on the degree of importance of particular facts, and they'd be there forever. Relationships between aspects of reality are similarly infinite in number, but if we first draw a circle around the aspect we wish to study, the number of relationships is reduced to a manageable level. Within that circle will be a network of relationships, some much more important than others. If a circle is drawn around, say, "trees," "thunderstorms," or "Tibetans," *systemic* relationships are enclosed, all of which are relevant.

This process, repeated, soon makes it clear that the task is to make sense of *systems*—a unified whole made up of interrelated elements. The relative importance of a particular system component is indicated by how much a change in it affects the rest of the system.

Galaxies are systems. Molecules are systems. And in between are systems to which we give more direct attention. Football teams are systems. Hurricanes are systems. Country clubs are systems. Flowering plants, supermarkets, sound amplifiers, viruses, corporations, legislatures, and airlines are systems. Within our bodies are skeletal systems, cardiovascular systems, muscular systems, digestive systems, respiratory systems, and so on (actually, of course, they're sub-systems of the larger system called "human organism").

Systems are what learners must understand, and that understanding comes from learners themselves investigating many different systems, looking for general principles. This requires (1) noting significant parts of the system being studied, (2) identifying important interrelationships among those parts, (3) deciding what forces are making the system operate, (4) noting the interactions between the system and its environment, and (5) tracking changes to the system over time.

These elements can be represented graphically (see Figure 2.1).

If learners apply these five general analytical categories, over and over, to systems of all sorts, the categories will give them a mental framework—a way of organizing what's being learned. That framework will, of course, be enhanced by the addition of appropriate analytical sub-categories expanding the learner's mental "filing system."

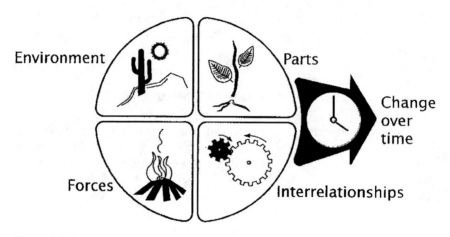

Figure 2.1.

Such a framework is missing from today's curriculum, and as a consequence learners are overwhelmed. In response to one of my Knight-Ridder/Tribune columns in the *Orlando Sentinel* newspaper about information overload, I got the following email from John Perry, a teacher in central Florida[1]:

Marion,

Your comments about the SSS [Florida's Sunshine State Standards] hit home for me this year because I ended up teaching middle school science. It is unbelievable what we are asked to do to our students. I expected that middle school science might be divided up into, say physical, earth, and life science in 6th, 7th, and 8th grade respectively. Well, no, even that would make too much sense. Sixth grade science is a survey course of...well, everything under the sun. We have a 776 page book loaded with very concentrated information. There are 23 chapters:

1. The Nature of Science
2. Measurement
3. Matter
4. Properties and Changes
5. Waves
6. Motion and Forces
7. Work and Simple Machines
8. Views of Earth
9. Resources
10. Atmosphere
11. Weather
12. Climate

13. Ecosystems
14. The Structure of Organisms
15. Classifying living things
16. Bacteria
17. Protists and Fungi
18. Plants
19. Plant Processes
20. Invertebrate Animals
21. Vertebrate Animals
22. Animal Behavior
23. The Solar System and Beyond

Whew! Seem like a tall order for sixth graders to absorb in one year? Even absurd? Yeah. Well, I'm on a block schedule. My students are expected to absorb all of this in ONE SEMESTER! And get this—the team I am on (myself, a math teacher, and a language arts teacher), was formed by taking the bottom third of the reading scores in sixth grade and putting all those kids together! How do you think they respond to this textbook, with its blizzard of unfamiliar vocabulary? These kids, who most need hands-on concept building, are expected instead to stand in front of a virtual fire hose of information and be blasted. (Please excuse the mixed metaphors!)

The district has two semester exams to diagnose how my students are doing. Soon, they will be tested on FCAT [Florida Comprehensive Achievement Test]. If they do poorly, the students, the school and I will be labeled failures. Well, there is definitely a failure here, but it isn't me or my kids.

John

There's a great deal wrong in the situation John describes. What's in that textbook isn't science but a sort of "science catechism," a compendium of information to be taught as revealed truth or expert opinion. That, of course, is contrary to the real spirit of science. But the most obvious problem is the volume and diversity of information learners are expected to absorb. Without any time for contemplation or for real, hands-on activity, it's a safe bet that little or nothing will make it into long-term memory, and even less will be understood well enough to be of practical use. What learners are most likely to take away from the course is either a dislike for the subject or the conclusion that it's hopelessly complex.

Simply using the common elements of systems—parts, interactions, forces, environment, change—when dealing with the phenomena laid out in John's science textbook would have been enormously helpful in efforts to make sense of it. It's still likely that much would soon be lost from memory, but the chances of retaining more of it would be improved because learners would have a "mental filing system" for storing information. Much more importantly, they'd have learned ways to handle and make sense of complex reality in any context.

At a common-sense level, everyone knows about causal sequences, connections, and systemic relationships. But making an understanding of them work for our individual and collective good requires a far more systematic approach to identifying the critically important systems within which they occur, then helping learners fashion the conceptual tools necessary for describing, analyzing, and altering them.

Which systems should be studied? In the final analysis, we want to survive, so it's a safe bet that most will agree that systems bearing on human life are Priority Number One, followed by those systems having to do with liberty and happiness. Abandoning the assumption that "covering the material" in the core subjects is the task, and focusing attention on relationships with implications for life, liberty, and happiness, would give general education the focus it presently lacks.

This may sound hopelessly theoretical, but it could hardly be more practical. Here's Henry Ford, in 1926, announcing a new policy based on his conception of what's necessary to make what might be called a "micro-economic" or "local economic" system work better:

> We have decided upon and at once put into effect through all the branches of our industries the five-day week. Hereafter there will be no more work on Saturdays and Sundays ...
>
> The industry of this country could not long exist if factories generally went back to the 10-hour day, because the people would not have the time to consume the goods produced. For instance, a workman would have little use for an automobile if he had to be in the shops from dawn until dusk. And that would react in countless directions, for the automobile, by enabling people to get about quickly and easily, gives them a chance to find out what is going on in the world—which leads them to a larger life that requires more food, more and better goods, more books, more music—more of everything.

Ford had previously demonstrated his understanding of causal sequences and systemic relationships. Twelve years earlier he'd started paying his workers the then unheard-of sum of five dollars for an eight-hour day. That was more than twice the industry average, which was two dollars and a half for a 10-hour day. If he wanted to sell a lot of cars, Ford reasoned, ordinary people had to make enough money to buy them.

Exploring relationships and systems requires a comprehensive, "master" organizer of knowledge that encompasses their infinite range, and an overarching aim for educating that narrows the focus of explorations to those bearing most directly on life, liberty, and happiness. On that foundation a true *discipline* can be built.

The systems most important to every individual—those that impact life at every moment—are systems in which *people* are the main components. Such systems supply our food, educate us; maintain our health; provide jobs, recreation, and ways of communicating; give us tools for travel and work; shape our laws; and bury us when we die.

Any of these systems may be analyzed and investigated using the five main analytical categories already described. However, when we focus on human systems, some refinement of the analytical categories will be helpful beyond simply identifying "people" as "system parts." We can still look at how the people within the system relate to each other and interact, and still trace relationships between the system and its environment, just as we do for non-human systems, but in the study of *human* systems, the primary driving forces are distinctive—the ideas or states of mind shared by members of the particular human group being studied.

This gives us all the elements of a new discipline, a new "master" organizer or model of reality that ties together and unifies the important dimensions of reality.

Here's what may come as a surprise: When we look at the five elements of this discipline, we discover that there's nothing really new there. A comprehensive, "supradisciplinary," systemically integrated discipline already exists.

CONSTRUCTING A SENSE-MAKING MODEL OF REALITY

People have been making sense of experience without fragmenting it and focusing on the fragments for as long as there have been people. As soon as infants are born, years before fourth or fifth grade when the education system begins to hammer them with separate subjects, the young are making good sense of experience. Billions of people unfamiliar with modern Western education's traditional (math–science–language arts–social studies) curriculum have managed to create and maintain complex, self-sufficient societies and civilizations.

Unfortunately, we aren't conscious of the fact that the knowledge-organizing system learners need already exists, indeed, is probably hard-wired in the brain.

That formal use has never been made of the system is best explained by the old saying, "A fish would be the last to discover water." The ubiquitous, the too-familiar, the always-there, lies in the unconscious mind and is all but invisible. Attention can be called to it, but that doesn't necessarily result in its "registering" or being seen as important. One can imagine Sir Isaac Newton's neighbors reacting to his excitement about gravity by saying he should go home and take a nap because they already knew—

everybody already knew—that apples, detached from trees, fall to the ground.

All humans have and make non-stop use of their hard-wired, knowledge-organizing and manipulating system, but when that system is pointed out, it's usually dismissed as too simple to be significant, and certainly not revolutionary in its potential for improving learner performance.

We have to get past this blindness stemming from over-familiarity. Every moment, in and out of school, the young are being bombarded with information. The brain selects from that flood of information, sorts and organizes it, and turns at least some of it into knowledge—perhaps even a little of it into wisdom. This happens on its own, but if the process is lifted into consciousness, studied, refined, and deliberate use is made of it, learners are able to perform at a whole new intellectual level.

We begin the sense-making process by pulling from the stream of consciousness something to think about—a happening, occurrence, situation, event, condition, state. Any matter will serve: "the Battle of Balaclava," "buying shoes," "Garden of Eden," "It's cold in here," "my funeral."

We locate what we're thinking about in time: "about mid-19th Century;" "Saturday morning," "a long time ago," "this moment," "three or four days after I die." (See Figure 2.2.)

We locate what we're thinking about in an environment: "Ukraine," "shoe store at the mall," "ancient Mesopotamia," "this room," "probably Greenlawn Cemetery." (See Figure 2.3.)

We identify the actors or participants: "British and Russians," "pushy salesman," "Adam and Eve," "me," "my relatives and friends." (See Figure 2.4.)

We describe or imagine the action: "Forward the Light Brigade!" "bought," "that snake and apple bit," "shivering," "standing around, maybe crying." (See Figure 2.5.)

We assume or postulate cause: "Threat to British sea routes," "needed shoes," "useful metaphor," "forgot my sweater," "I died." (See Figure 2.6.)

Finally, we integrate these five elements systemically to create our model of a particular reality. (See Figure 2.7.)

These are the basic organizing concepts of our comprehensive, "supradisciplinary," sense-making discipline, the tool we use to construct meaning: "I needed a pair of shoes, so last Saturday I went to that store in the mall where the pushy salesman works and bought a pair."

A simple exercise can demonstrate this knowledge-organizing system's ubiquitousness. Simply ask learners to collect several short newspaper articles, then ask: "What different *kinds* of information are in each article?" Perhaps unaccustomed to such an assignment, they may struggle a

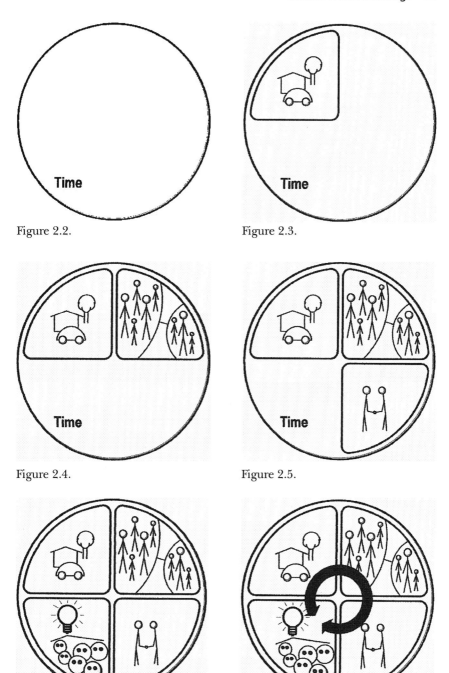

Figure 2.2.

Figure 2.3.

Figure 2.4.

Figure 2.5.

Figure 2.6.

Figure 2.7.

bit, but will eventually identify the standard elements—time, environment, actors, action, cause.

Simple, obvious stuff this. Those five kinds of information combine to create newspaper articles, novels, police reports, plays, research, myths, hopes, jokes, dreams, diaries, history books, policy documents, bedtime stories, legislation, conversation. They're the tools we use to shape our economy, political institutions, laws, ways of acting, art, architecture, hopes for the future. Everything we know—all street knowledge, all common sense, every academic discipline, every school subject, every lesson— is constructed from the five. And everything we'll ever know that we don't now know will have its origin in the discovery and exploration of relationships among their sub-categories, sub-sub-categories, and so on. We bundle the five together, bring them to bear on the reality "out there," and use them to construct a map or model of the "out there," "in here," in our heads.

The model in our heads, of course, will be much simpler than that which it models. There's no getting around that. Everything, even the simplest object, is too complex to be understood in a total sense. A dining room chair may seem ordinary enough, but from the standpoint of engineering design, component composition, or molecular structure, it's very complex. If we had to really understand the chair before we sat down, it wouldn't get used. We're able to function because we create simple mental models of the things we think about and substitute those versions for the real thing. Road maps are models. So are recipes, computer simulations, chemical formulas, graphs, medical diagnoses, blueprints, psychological profiles, games of Monopoly. Everything we think about, we model.

Our mental models, of course, vary enormously in quality. A good model of spatial relationships in the solar system makes it possible to orbit Saturn with a spacecraft. Poor models of personality formation keep us from developing penal systems that decrease antisocial behavior. Good models of traffic flow allow traffic lights to be timed to minimize congestion. Poor models of the economy leave us uncertain about the causes and cures of inflation and depression. Good models will predict the flight characteristics of an aircraft still in the design stage, the reaction of a particular type of cancer cell to a proposed treatment, the response of a foreign government to a policy initiative.

The final test of a model's quality is the accuracy with which it describes what will happen in reality. Good models answer all relevant questions, including those we neglect to ask.

Our senses expose us to the real world in all its incredible complexity; we model it, and the model shapes the curriculum. The curriculum we must have if we're to adequately educate must model the whole of knowledge well enough to allow us to sort the significant from the insignificant, establish priorities, trace causal sequences, and imagine probable, possible, and preferable futures. Constructing that curriculum involves a transition that's usually easy for kids but hard for adults—moving from merely knowing, to knowing what we know, then knowing *how* we know what we know. The transition allows us to work on the quality of our model, consciously and deliberately, for the rest of our lives. How well we do that determines in large measure the quality of our lives—how usefully we interpret the past, how well we manage the present, how precisely we predict the future.

The difference in intellectual performance when learners surface and make deliberate use of the five-element Model of reality—when they make the familiar strange enough to see—is spectacular. Learners who learn to identify *for themselves* the five kinds of knowledge that organize the Model, who then elaborate and refine the five and explore their systemic relationships, will function at academic levels not now even being considered possible. Their superior performance may not be apparent on standardized tests, but it will be obvious in what really matters—in their improved ability to make sense of experience, and their increased levels of insight and creativity.

In simplest terms, the Model is a template that, laid down on particular experience, identifies information and sorts it out to make the most possible sense of it, no matter if that experience is an historical event, the daily round of life, the first day on a new job, a dispute between neighbors or nations, the culture of a primitive tribe, "those people on the other side of the railroad tracks," or the possible unintended consequences of a proposed piece of legislation. The template says, "If you want to understand what you're thinking about as completely and as thoroughly as possible, you need to know this, this, this, and this. And you need to know how they relate."

As most readers will already have noted, the Model is just an elaborated version of what middle school newspaper staffs are told by their supervising teachers in their first meetings, that a proper news story includes the relevant information about who, what, when, where, and why.

With that realization usually comes skepticism. It's hard to accept that a knowledge organizer routinely used by everybody, including small children—an organizer so familiar, so natural—if lifted into consciousness, elaborated, and deliberately used, could revolutionize learner performance. Surely, if it had that potential, it would long ago have been pointed out and put to work!

Skepticism was the reaction of most reviewers of the manuscript of *What's Worth Teaching?* in which this idea was laid out in 1988. That manuscript, submitted to the State University of New York Press, was distributed by SUNY editors to reviewers, along with a form asking nine questions, followed by space for comment, and concluding with blanks for checkmarks on a six-point scale ranging from "Outstanding" to "Unpublishable."

The first review returned began with the words, "It would be difficult to call this a scholarly work," and ended with a checkmark in the space in front of the word "Unpublishable," the lowest mark on the scale. Another early reviewer sent the manuscript back to editors with, "Almost pure schlock!" scrawled in large script across the last page. This reviewer concurred with the first and put a checkmark before "Unpublishable."

But other reviewers and SUNY Press editors came to a different conclusion, so *What's Worth Teaching?* was published. However, most educators still don't see merit in a general education curriculum that uses the elements of the Model rather than school subjects and courses as its primary organizer. Such a curriculum must be legitimized by authority, and that hasn't happened. Indeed, the "standards and accountability" fad that began about the same time as the book was published assured it would be ignored.

Further elaboration of the major elements of the Model may help make more apparent its ability to encompass, organize, and systemically integrate reality. In the discussions that follow, keep in mind that the aim isn't just to create a comprehensive, systemically integrated discipline, but to make that discipline easily understood and easy to use.

Consistent with that aim, terms and labels for the Model's five major components will be the simplest available and in common use: Time, Environment, Actors, Action, and Shared Ideas.

As you read, it will help make the five more manageable if they're applied to a specific *system* or *systems*—organized human groups such as particular societies, peoples, subcultures, ethnic groups, tribes—or other organized, coherent groups, including your own, and to specific, happenings, events, occurrences, situations, states, conditions, circumstances.

Concreteness makes for understanding, but there's a second, extremely important reason for making organized human groups the primary focus of study and illustration: They're the generators of systems of meaning or "sense." Viewing the same reality, but from a different cultural or societal perspective, means that what makes sense in one doesn't necessarily make sense in another. There *is* no "culture free" perspective, not even in math and science. There may be agreement about "the facts," but that doesn't mean there's agreement about their relative importance or the role they should play in human affairs.

Here, again, are the main elements of the Model:

- **Time:** Information about time—frequency, duration, etc.—of what's being thought about

Figure 2.8.

- **Environment:** Information about the focus of attention, the actual environment of the happening, occurrence, event, state, condition, etc.
- **Actors:** Information about the participants—their number, age, gender, and so on
- **Action:** Information about the actual movement and behavior of the actors
- **Shared Ideas:** Information about the beliefs, values, assumptions, and other states of mind of the actors
- **Relationships:** Relevant information about how environment, actors, action, and shared ideas relate systemically

"Relevant" information is information that, if it were different, would change the happening in some significant way. For example, a party attended by the same people will be a different experience if held on a public beach or in a private home. Double or halve the number of actors and it will again be a very different experience. Change the shared idea for the party from a long-awaited reunion to a last get-together before a permanent parting, and the experience changes again.

For the sake of convenience, in the following discussions, environment, actors, action, shared ideas, and their relationships, will usually be pulled together in the context of "social systems," or "societies," and the template guiding the description and analysis of such systems will be called "Model."

In the context of these systems, the major elements of the Model will be examined in greater detail to demonstrate their comprehensiveness. It should become clear not only that no content traditionally taught as part of the general education curriculum is being slighted, but also that the Model pulls in additional content of undeniable relevance to sense making.

ENVIRONMENT

Imagine a vast shopping mall, open for business, colored lights playing on a central fountain, neon signs flashing, merchandise stacked on shelves and racks, climate control system maintaining temperature and humidity, cash registers and computers turned on and warm—and no human anywhere. Move outside into a warm summer evening, to a parking lot filled with empty automobiles, then beyond to streets where more empty cars sit with engines running. Traffic signals change but no cars move. Telephones function, but no one calls. Television screens display test patterns or taped images, but there are no viewers. Out on the edge of the city, empty airplanes sit on lighted runways, radar antennas rotating but no one interpreting the data. Diesel locomotives attached to strings of freight and tank cars stand in switch-yards with engines idling, but there's no human presence.

Figure 2.9.

These are the elements of a place, a familiar, urban American environment. It's a stage with props, a space with equipment, a setting, a place where people pursue a way of life. Every society occupies space, and the nature of that space—its size, shape, climate, resources, tools, and other accumulated paraphernalia of the past that fill it—bend, mold, and stamp those within the space, organizing their lives, defining their problems, shaping their creativity, limiting their dreams.

Environment: Constructions

Houses used to have attics. The residue of generations accumulated there, and on rainy days children could spend hours with objects and items belonging to parents, grandparents, and other family members. Clothes, scrapbooks, toys, photographs, and much else could be looked at, tried on, played with, studied.

Many newer houses don't have attics. They increase construction costs. Most roofs are now supported by light-weight trusses which make the use of attic space more difficult. The objects and items which might once have found their way to the attic are now usually discarded—given away, set out to be picked up by the trash collector, or saved for a time and then sold at a garage sale.

Does such a minor change in the shape of a particular small place make any difference? It may. The difference may be subtle, but surely it exists. The child who spends long afternoons in an attic carefully scrutinizing and touching evidence that his or her parents were once also small, that they played with toys, wrote in childish scrawls, won trophies, valued certain useless things—surely that child is different, albeit in some indefinable way, from the child whose environment testifies that only the present is tangible and valued.

The houses and neighborhoods of eighty or so years ago and those of the present differ in other ways. The glass in the front door, once constituting most of its area, has shrunk to the size of a tiny button or has been entirely eliminated. The front porch is often gone, and with it the porch furniture. Clotheslines have been replaced by dryers. Alleys are no longer considered an economical use of space, so in all but upscale subdivisions, developers leave them out. Heating and cooling systems create steady background noises that blot out the sounds of the neighborhood. Garages are attached, and remote-controlled doors make it possible to leave and enter with a minimum of human contact. There are fewer vacant lots, fewer paths to isolation, fewer places of natural danger. The shape of environments has changed, and every change has made a difference in how those within them relate to the world, to each other, and to themselves.

It isn't just the shape of neighborhoods that affects the nature of human experience. World history textbooks teach that the history of ancient Greece was in part a product of the rugged terrain of the Greek peninsula. Appalachia and other parts of the United States where access is more difficult tend to change more slowly than other regions. Research indicates that ceiling height, wall color, and other physical features of a room directly affect emotions and actions. Longtime operators of bars know that seating arrangement, booth style, restroom location, and many other design features affect in important ways the length of customer stay, the likelihood of altercations, and money spent.

Hundreds of department stores have gone to great expense to relocate escalators less conveniently, changing traffic patterns to increase customer exposure to "impulse items." Jane Jacobs, Edward T. Hall, and others have shown that length of city block, street width, parking lot dimensions, building heights, office design, and just about every other feature of physical environments contribute in powerful ways not just to action but to feeling and thought.

This isn't an esoteric, marginally important subject. The shape of places has an enormous impact on family relationships, neighboring networks, crime and violence, educational effectiveness, business success, and almost every other aspect of daily life. One would suppose, then, that a study of the relationships between humans and the shapes of the places they occupy and create would be thoroughly explored in general education, but the matter is rarely even mentioned.

Environment: Resources

The young Asian girl stands facing a sun-warmed brick wall not far from the commercial heart of the village. She stoops, acquires a large handful of dung from a bucket, and plasters it neatly on the wall to dry. The geometric pattern she creates spans from ground level to as far as she can reach and back to her left to where the wall turns a corner. A small boy brings another container and the pattern lengthens. The dried cakes of dung will fuel family fires for cooking and for night-time warmth.

"Resources" can be an unwieldy concept. One group's pollution can be the mainstay of another group's economy. One era's resource base lies, in another era, unused and unwanted. That which seems to have no value can become, because of technological changes, almost invaluable. The resource picture can be relatively simple, as it is for those groups that require little more than grazing land and water. Or it can be complex, with resource needs encompassing most minerals and energy sources.

Adults who attended elementary school before the study of geography was abandoned may be able to name the major resources upon which the economies of several nations depend. But a simple cataloging of resources is of little benefit in making sense of a particular way of life. It's *relationships* that matter, relationships between a people's resources and their states of mind, between their resources and their patterns of action, between their resources and their demographic characteristics. Some of those relationships are so direct and obvious there's hardly room for discussion, but others aren't at all apparent. Those are the ones to which the Model can call attention.

As the world begins to face the hard facts of oil depletion and climate change, learners and the rest of us need conceptual tools for anticipating and coping with their society-shattering potential. The Model can provide those tools.

Environment: Climate

In the early 1900s, Ellsworth Huntington, a professor of geography at Yale, argued that the rise and fall of civilizations followed a six-hundred-year cycle. He thought that when global changes in climate blessed for a time a particular region of the earth, productivity and power for the people of that region followed. It's not that simple, of course, but as is increasingly apparent, climatic changes impact ways of life in all sorts of unexpected ways.

The first great civilizations of Sumer and Egypt formed during a period beginning about eight thousand years ago known as the Climatic Optimum. The later trends in climate that changed the Fertile Crescent to desert were surely a factor in the demise of those civilizations. It's likely a period of cooling that, beginning about 2,000 B.C., pushed Hittites, Medes, Aryans, and Dorians south as invaders. Later, climate cooperated as Greece and Rome rose to power. The southward movement of Germanic tribes that overthrew Rome coincided with increasing harshness of climate in northern Europe.

Pleasant climate brought prosperous, food-producing colonies to Greenland and Newfoundland, and the advancing cold of the Little Ice Age appears to have destroyed them. That era ended about 1875. Since then, the warmest weather in the last four thousand years has prevailed. In this era industrialization has peaked, America's population has more than doubled, and food production has expanded again and again.

Individuals are aware of immediate climate conditions and perhaps of relatively short-term trends over a few years, but unaided memory is too short and the physical senses too imprecise to register variations that, although seemingly minor, may have significant consequences.

Long-term cycles of sunspot activity, increases in volcanic eruptions, atmospheric changes due to industrial or commercial activity—as most now understand, these can alter the earth's climate with consequences, some of which aren't yet apparent. Even the most conservative estimates of increases in Earth's temperature, if they come to pass, will dramatically alter ways of life.

Attention is paid to global warming, but it seems fair to say that the general education curriculum isn't doing much to prepare the young for adapting to the life-style changes it will necessitate.

Environment: Tools

How technological changes affect ways of life gets considerable attention in historical study. Most students have been told how the compass, cotton gin, computer, and other major inventions changed society. In fact, technology as a factor in social change may get so much attention that other causes of change may be overshadowed.

But widespread awareness of the role of technology in triggering change doesn't mean that the *process* is understood, or that its subtleties and ramifications are appreciated. What the Model offers beyond usual study is a comprehensive means of tracing the *range* of effects of an innovation and the often-complicated, many-stage causal sequences it often triggers.

The transition from steam to diesel locomotives during World War II as described by W.F. Cotrell in an article in the June, 1951 issue of the *American Sociological Review* illustrates the vast and varied consequences that can result from a single innovation. In order to move the millions of tons of war materials needed overseas during the war, the United States found it necessary to build large numbers of ocean-going freighters. Many of these ships were designed for diesel engines, with the result that facilities for the production of large diesels had to be rapidly and extensively expanded.

At the same time, the movement of goods and military personnel by rail within the United States was placing heavy demands on the available steam locomotives. Partly because large diesel engines were becoming available, and partly because diesels were cheaper to operate, steam locomotives began to be replaced by diesel units.

The social effects of this change were far-reaching. The pre-World War II locomotive demanded extensive routine maintenance. For some procedures, the locomotive had to be disconnected from the train, an operation that required men and equipment. Since the train had to stop anyway, cars were inspected and shunted into a shop for repair. These operations required additional men, heavy equipment, and facilities. Around these railroad service points towns grew, towns in which the biggest payroll and the largest property taxes were paid by the railroad. With the railroad shops providing a seemingly secure economic base, political institutions were created; stores, banks, and other businesses were established; and populations expanded. Towns stabilized around the economy of the railroad.

But diesel locomotives changed everything. Needing far fewer stops for fuel and service, trains passed through dozens of railroad towns without pausing. Railroad shops shut down, payrolls ended abruptly, and people moved away. Banks and other businesses closed their doors. Schools and churches were boarded up. Civic clubs disbanded, and lawyers, physicians, and other professionals established practices elsewhere. Many of the towns deserted by the railroads never recovered.

The changes accompanying the transition from steam to diesel locomotives were startlingly swift, but they weren't unique. Indeed, it's difficult to think of a technological innovation that hasn't altered life in some way. Analyzing the impacts of such changes, the Model helps pull thinking on from a preoccupation with the innovation itself to its direct and indirect consequences. It can make far more apparent how change structures and restructures daily routine, creates individual and societal problems, renders skills and abilities obsolete, turns assets into liabilities, drives economic and psychological wedges between individuals and between groups, undermines institutional effectiveness, and generates vast social and psychological stress.

Environment: Wealth

An old saying has it that money can't buy happiness. However, money can and does buy differing experiences, and those differing experiences can have much to do not only with happiness but with much else of consequence.

Consider, for example, some of the infant and childhood experiences a middle-class level of wealth can buy, as pointed out by historian David Potter in his 1954 book, *People of Plenty*, published by the University of Chicago Press:

- Birth and early care in a technologically complex hospital
- The technology and equipment for bottle feeding

- A separate crib or bed
- Diapers and other devices permitting permissive toilet training
- Warmth through space heating rather than by freedom-constricting swaddling
- A room of one's own, often with amenities such as television
- Parents who've chosen when and how many children to have
- Separate housing, away from grandparents and other members of the extended family
- Insulation from survival concerns such as food, clothing, and shelter
- Exclusive ownership of toys and other objects
- Travel
- The services of doctors, dentists, music teachers, etc.

It's relatively easy to see possible relationships between these kinds of socialization experiences and some important ideas shared by adult Americans. Deep-seated attitudes about individualism, freedom, equality, competitiveness, mobility, and democracy are consistent with and no doubt have roots in childhood experiences related to material abundance. In more subtle but equally powerful ways, differing levels of wealth within and between human societies help create differing conceptions of the self, others, how the "good life" is defined, how families are organized, friends made, creativity expressed, and decisions made.

What might be called "system wealth"—assets that flow rather freely among individuals and groups—is usually related to resources but isn't the same thing. The fertile soil of North America was a resource to the colonists but of somewhat less direct value to many Indian tribes. The colonists made use of water power to grind grain and power sawmills and forges, but ignored the coal and oil upon which America's economy later became dependent. As some Asian societies have demonstrated, it's possible to generate enormous quantities of system wealth without much of a foundation of natural wealth.

The study of wealth—the total amount within a society's setting, its distribution, and its impact on that society's way of life—belongs in the general education curriculum, and the Model puts it there.

Environment: Alien Organisms and Substances

In ancient Rome, the wealthy leadership classes ate on glazed earthenware and drank water carried in lead pipe. Some historians think the decline of Rome could be blamed in part on the leadership's loss of mental ability as the lead gradually affected their ability to think.

In 1349, English authorities imposed an ordinance requiring that everyone work for the same pay as they'd received two years earlier. There were penalties for refusal to work, penalties for leaving a job to take another one for higher pay, and penalties for employers who offered pay increases to their employees. Parliament was attempting, unsuccessfully, to combat one of the effects of the Black Plague. So many workers had died that those who were left found themselves in good bargaining positions. It isn't too far-fetched to argue that the Plague helped eliminate feudalism.

When average scores on the Scholastic Aptitude Test began to decline in the 1960s, some researchers said the main reason was Iodine-131. Test takers, they said, had been born during the era of atmospheric testing of nuclear devices, and enough of the element had been absorbed to affect the thyroid gland's production of hormones controlling brain development.

Obviously, ways of life can be much altered by organisms and substances. Sometimes the effects are immediate and obvious, as was the case when Ireland was struck by the potato blight in mid-19th century. In a very short period of time, Irish ways of life radically changed. For example, the average age for marrying quickly changed from one of the earliest in the Western world to one of the latest. More often, however, changes caused by alien organisms and substances occur so gradually they're not even noticed, or become apparent so late that effective reaction is impossible. Asbestos fibers in the air, mercury in fish, lead in automobile exhaust gases, acid in rain, water hyacinth in lakes and rivers, food additives in the digestive system—we know about and watch at least some elements that can alter relationship between aspects of reality and the way systems function, but in general, too little attention is paid. The Model raises awareness of seemingly minor environmental changes that can have major long-term consequences, and calls attention to their relationship to each other and to ways of life.

ACTORS

The day's news of the world is dominated by references to groups—Americans, Canadians, Tibetans, Israelis, Ugandans, and so on. These groups are held together—sometimes tightly, sometimes very loosely—by custom, social institutions, laws, belief systems, common interests, and other ties. Making sense of the actions and interactions of those within the group, and of their interactions with other groups, requires description

Figure 2.10.

and analysis. Failure to adequately understand or interpret information about actors can literally be deadly. Making good sense of that information vastly increases the likelihood of success in humankind's striving for life, liberty, and happiness.

Actors: Number

The aspects of reality of major concern in general education are those involving people. From their number in any given situation, much follows. Schools with fifty students will differ in myriad and fundamental ways from schools with five hundred or five thousand students. The same will be true of corporations, tribes, neighborhoods, and nations. The size of membership will affect every major aspect of a particular system's internal dynamics and external relationships.

Establishing the number of members in a system may be easy—perhaps as simple as counting all individuals wearing a particular uniform or residing in an isolated valley. However, deciding who does and who doesn't belong to a particular system is often rather difficult. Race, color, and place of residence or occupation don't necessarily establish membership. What counts are shared ways of acting and states of mind. Counting is also complicated by the fact that several different systems often occupy the same general area and share many ways of acting and ideas. Boundaries can be very fuzzy. What's seen as a system also depends in part on what one is attempting to understand—a family, work team, social class, ethnic minority, primitive tribe, or, in rare instances, a nation. The Japanese come close to being a nation that's also a coherent system or society, but Americans don't. Hell's Angels and the Amish are Americans, but there's a considerable difference in their actions and shared ideas.

Actors: Age

How many hospital rooms or outboard motors are going to be needed in seven years? What tendencies in the crime rate can be expected? How many contributors to the social security system will there be in the next generation? Are more or fewer doctors going to be required? In what direction is the general political orientation of the country likely to evolve? What will happen to the sales of a particular make of automobile given its image in the minds of various age groups?

Information about the relative number of individuals in various age groups can help answer an enormous range of questions. In all systems, each age group has a variety of tendencies, characteristics, responsibilities, interests, roles, and problems that translate into ways of acting. One age group will be unproductive and dependent. Another will be involved in instruction for adulthood. Others will be consumers of certain kinds of goods or services—will be in need of dwelling space, work animals, insurance, tools, or "the latest hit single." Others will be expected to fight, to give a period of time to public service, fulfill a religious responsibility, or bear children.

Because the actions of each age group create certain demands, generate peculiar problems, drain certain resources, require special facilities, expand certain capabilities, or limit certain potentials, information about the actual and relative size of age subgroups or those in various life stages is essential. Information about the size of age groups approaching different life stages is also of great value.

Actors: Gender

Members of groups in which the ratio between females and males has long remained unchanged are likely to have little awareness of the extent that actions and shared ideas are geared to the prevailing sex ratio. It's only when a long-prevailing ratio changes, or when another system or society with a differing ratio is studied, that the far-reaching ramifications of the relative number of each sex become apparent. If nature was the only operative factor, and the balance between the number of male and female births was always relatively constant, there might be less reason to include information about that ratio on the Model. But balance is by no means ensured. War is a major creator of gender imbalance in many groups. In others, the pursuit of a livelihood, the search for adventure, or adherence to a religious precept may create major or minor differences in the number of males and females. There's also the various means by which parents can determine the gender of those born, with resultant social ramifications stemming from their choices.

Whatever the situation—balanced, unbalanced, static, or changing—the sexual ratio within a system has such an impact, and affects in such myriad ways other elements of the system, prevailing and potential ratios must be known and their implications understood.

Actors: Distribution

To the traveler rounding a bend on a rural road in Europe, a dozen or so buildings will often appear, closely packed, houses and sheds almost leaning against each other. The road may narrow, zig-zag between the buildings, then open up once more to a countryside with no structure visible anywhere.

Along the highways of Indiana, Illinois, and much of the rest of the rural American Midwest, the scene is different. Isolated houses stand in the centers of farms or sit alone by the road, often far beyond convenient walking distance to the next house.

The difference is important. In myriad, subtle ways, patterns of action and interaction and the shared ideas and feelings accompanying those actions are in part a product of the distribution and density of the population. Is it clustered in groups? Concentrated in a single, compact area? Ranged along the banks of a river or the edge of a forest? Shelved on the levels of high-rise structures or ringing an oasis?

Density and distribution of population don't necessarily determine lifestyles or institutions, but they exert considerable influence toward certain kinds of interactions and make other kinds of interaction difficult. It wouldn't be likely that the population of an area in rural Wyoming could assemble a symphony orchestra, or that the residents of Manhattan could organize to provide their own food supply. Ways of relating, organizing for action, dividing work and responsibility, controlling deviance, expressing creativity, educating the young—collective and individual effort is shaped in part by the number of others involved and their physical distance from each other.

Information about the number, age, sex, distribution, density, and inherent physical or mental capacities and capabilities of those who together constitute a system is the second major component of the Model.

Figure 2.11

ACTION

In a Bedouin camp, a child calls attention to a camel approaching in the distance. The men and children congregate in front of one of the tents to watch the arrival, while the women and older girls hurry away, out of sight in the women's section. The man on the camel is identified as a Bedouin by his clothing—a red checkered headcloth held by a rope, a long white shirt, a dark brown cloak. Even at a distance, however, he's recognized as a stranger, for he wears his long hair braided and he rides sitting high on the center of the camel's hump rather than farther back as is the local custom. He approaches from the south, for that's the direction toward which the tents open, and even though the terrain is level, he follows a slow, zig-zag course, showing first his left side to the observers, then his right.

The Bedouin participants in this brief human encounter almost certainly aren't aware of the eight patterns involved in the encounter. To them, a stranger has arrived in a proper way. Even if they're familiar with patterns for arrival used by those in other systems, they're still not likely to "stand above" themselves, look down at familiar ways of acting, and see them as patterns.

The same is true of the members of any group. It's hard to make the familiar strange enough to see clearly and objectively. Not only are the patterned actions too close to be apparent; they're hedged about with unspoken, unexplored assumptions about what's right and proper, and complicated by the symbolism attached to some of them.

Of the thousands of patterns routinely followed by the members of a society, relatively few are really important. Whether or not the members of a system eat with fingers or forks, drive on the left or the right, shake hands or bow when greeting, makes little difference. The genuinely significant action patterns are those which, if they change, reach out and alter other ways of acting, actors, environment, or shared ideas. For example, a decision to produce goods in a way that requires division of labor will have revolutionary, and generally unanticipated, consequences. The adoption of remote electronic shopping, the practice of isolating the elderly or actively integrating them, the custom of marrying at a particular age or having families of certain sizes, are other general actions that ripple through a system affecting much else.

In any attempt to make more sense of a human system, the important ways of acting within it must be noted. It's essential to know who ordinarily does what, with whom, how frequently, for how long, where, with what—general questions, yes, but questions requiring precise answers if the nature of human experience is to be understood.

Action: Socializing

In every society, the members have at least some free time, time when choices can be made about whom to be with and under what circumstances. Differences in patterns for associating vary enormously from group to group, and may also vary considerably over time within the same group, but patterns there will be.

A too-little-appreciated example of the latter can be found in relatively recent American history. For many elderly Americans, patterns for socializing during their early years frequently, maybe almost always, put them in contact with others whose ages spanned from early infancy to old age. They attended small schools where ages in a single room may have ranged from five or six to the late teen years. In small rural churches they sat in congregations where infants in arms and the elderly were ordinarily in attendance. At social activities, community suppers, games, work parties, and when hunting, for example, they shared the activity with participants of all ages.

The picture has changed radically. Rarely are children in school now in the same classroom with those whose ages differ more than a year or two from their own. Large religious organizations ordinarily segregate by age. Little League sports and dozens of other forms of recreation involve individuals of closely bracketed age groups. In less than a hundred years, America has transformed from a society in which most patterns for socializing cut across all age groups, to a society in which nearly all patterns for associating are rather narrowly circumscribed by age. No important aspect of American life has remained untouched by that change. Its implications and ramifications are vast.

In every system or society, questions about who spends unstructured time with whom, doing what, when, where, with what, are essential to understanding. The Model takes note.

Action: Working

Out of the driveway at 7:13 … wave goodbye to daughter, Cindy, still in upstairs bedroom getting ready for school … eight blocks, two stop signs and one traffic signal to Outer Belt expressway ramp … six miles to north-south expressway ramp. 7:35 … one and a quarter miles to the off-ramp at 49th Street … bumper to bumper for the last seven blocks to the office … parking lot closed for paving …

One of the more intriguing aspects of computer technology is its potential for changing work patterns. For some, those changes have already begun. They work at home, the product of their labor converted to electrical pulses and transmitted elsewhere. "Elsewhere" may be across town, to a nearby city, or a point hundreds or thousands of miles away. "Going to work" means going into the bedroom or a corner of the kitchen. "The old 8 to 5" may be from 6 until 10, 2 until 4, or after the kids are in bed. The car stays in the garage. The worker doesn't visit the office because there *is* no office, no executive restroom, no drinking fountain, no parking lot, no file cabinets, no Christmas party, no hierarchy of supervisors and managers, no company cafeteria.

All the world's work can't, of course, be done on a computer. But a growing percentage of it can, and the number of individuals involved in that work is likely to grow very large, large enough to change traffic, change neighborhoods, change marital relationships, change parent–child relationships.

Changes in patterns for work nearly always have revolutionary consequences. Cottage industry, the use of animals, the factory system, division of labor, the eight-hour day and forty-hour week, minimum wage laws, apprenticeship, mandatory retirement, child labor laws, the number of workers required for a task, starting and stopping times, location—each pattern for work has consequences and implications that reach out and affect ideas, attitudes, and ways of life.

Action: Educating

In at least some Native American tribes, grandfathers were responsible for teaching grandsons. The two of them might spend extended periods away from camp following the trail of game, making tools and weapons, trapping, coping with weather—the grandfather demonstrating, explaining, testing; the grandson watching, listening, practicing. One can assume that, generally speaking, it was a way of educating that worked. Both teacher and learner realized the importance of the task and both probably found it rewarding and fulfilling.

The arrangement for educating worked well because the grandfather knew just about everything the grandson needed to know. His survival was proof of that. He knew the territory—land, animals, elements, enemies, problems, and their possibilities. Because the problems the grandson would encounter would be more or less identical to those the grandfather had already encountered, there wasn't much doubt that what was being transmitted from one generation to the next was valid and useful. The pattern for educating worked.

But eventually it stopped working, and the major reason illustrates why the Model is so important. Patterns need to be identified, understood, and evaluated by those caught up in them, and the Model raises awareness. The grandfather-knows-best pattern stopped working for most Native Americans when the knowledge needed for survival was no longer known by the grandfathers. What many Native Americans eventually came to need wasn't primarily an understanding of nature but an understanding of the intricacies of civil law. They needed to know about treaties, contracts, mineral rights, severance taxes, depletion allowances, and all the other provisions of the law touching on the holding, use, and management of their territory. Grandfather didn't have that information. Sometimes younger people did. At that point, a refusal to change the traditional pattern for educating could become (and in many cases actually was) the first step toward cultural destruction.

Educating isn't a single pattern, of course, but a complex of patterns having to do with who's taught what, by whom, where, how, when, with what—a great many variables, but every one of them important. Left alone, ways of educating get more and more out of sync with system survival needs, eventually either imploding from irrelevance or turning into expensive but meaningless rituals.

Action: Controlling Behavior

Colin Turnbull, an English anthropologist, lived for extended periods of time with the BaMbuti tribe of Pygmies in the Ituri Forest in Uganda. When the Pygmies made camp, he said, families constructed dwellings by bending green saplings to make a dome-shaped skeleton, weaving vines around the skeleton to make a latticework, and then covering the structure with mongongo leaves placed like tiles. Sometimes, Turnbull said, when a member of the tribe had acted in a way the other members of the tribe considered objectionable, those living nearby would reorient the entrances to their dwellings so as to point away from the one occupied by the offender. When behavior was acceptable, entrances were returned to their original location.

This somewhat unusual pattern of behavior is one of thousands devised by humans to encourage acceptable behavior. The requirement that Hester Prynne wear a scarlet letter on the front of her dress in Nathaniel Hawthorne's novel by that name was another approach. Gossip, ridicule, electrocution, banishment, ostracism, imprisonment, public hanging, excommunication, stretching on the rack, fingerprinting, derision, and fines also have that purpose. Sometimes rewards, prizes, bonuses, compliments, and promises are employed for the same reason.

Most members of most systems follow most of the action patterns of the systems to which they belong for reasons other than fear of the methods used to control deviance. Most often, of course, individuals do as they do because alternatives haven't occurred to them or, if they have, the alternatives aren't appealing. Adherence to patterns also frequently stems from beliefs about the expectations of others or of supernatural beings. Custom, habit, belief—whatever the first cause for adhering to prevailing patterns—the need to conform is communicated to the members of societies in many different ways.

Ways of controlling deviance is important. If they don't work well, the system becomes unstable and may come apart. Each member must be able to predict with considerable accuracy how other members are going to act and react in every situation. It's necessary, for example, to believe that the drivers of oncoming automobiles are going to do everything in their power to honor the pattern and stay in their traffic lane. The whole world functions primarily because people go where they're expected to go, at approximately the expected time, and do what they're expected to do.

Action patterns for controlling deviance can, however, work too well. To survive, systems have to constantly adapt to changing circumstances, which frequently requires replacing old patterns with new ones. But long-repeated actions tend to take on an aura of sacredness, causing those who attempt new ways of acting to be viewed negatively. If the techniques for controlling deviance are too effective, or not effective enough, the results can destroy the system. History is full of examples, not often recognized, of patterns for controlling deviance so rigidly adhered to that necessary adaptation was impossible.

Tracing a path between instability and rigidity is one of the most complex challenges systems face, and societies in which the problem isn't understood are poorly equipped to deal with it. The Model directs attention to the matter.

Action: Distributing Wealth

In Thomas Jefferson's autobiography, he describes a project begun in 1777 to "create a system of laws" for the new state of Virginia. Jefferson was one of a committee of five appointed by the legislature and given responsibility for the task. He wrote as follows:

> I proposed to abolish the law of primogeniture, and to make real estate descendible in parcenary to the next of kin, as personal property now is, by the statute of distribution. Mr. Pendleton wished to preserve the right of primogeniture, but seeing at once that could not prevail, he proposed we should adopt the Hebrew principle, and give a double portion to the elder son. I observed, that if the eldest son could eat twice as much or do twice the work, it might be natural evidence of his right to a double portion; but being on a par in his powers and wants, with his brothers and sisters, he should be on a par also in the partition of the patrimony.

Jefferson and the four members of his committee understood and appreciated the importance of patterns for distributing wealth. They knew that acceptance of the principle of primogeniture would be followed by the creation of one sort of society and way of life, and rejecting the pattern would create another, very different society. If an estate passed intact from oldest son to oldest son, a permanent class of landed gentry would be created, and social, economic, and political power would tend to concentrate in their hands. If, on the other hand, all heirs were treated equally, wealth would tend to be in constant movement and would be more accessible to those of ability regardless of their order of birth. Equality of opportunity would be fostered. Jefferson once said he didn't think it was possible for a legislature to pass too many laws dividing up property.

All societies develop powerful emotional attachments to their major ways of acting. To patterns for distributing wealth, this attachment is almost always particularly strong. Capitalism is a pattern for distributing wealth, and emotion about it often runs high. "From each according to his ability, to each according to his need," is a description of another pattern for distributing wealth. The pattern for distributing wealth called "feudalism" ordered much of the life of medieval Europe. Robin Hood's fame derived in part from his promotion of a particular pattern for redistributing wealth.

Large-scale patterns for distributing wealth aren't the only ones of significance. In some societies, all family members, including grown children, pool their incomes. In others, each member of the family keeps possession and control of his or her own earnings. In some groups, alms giving and receiving are of significance in the distribution of wealth. In others, the practice is almost unknown.

Patterns for distributing wealth aren't, as Karl Marx maintained, all-pervasive. They don't determine all other patterns. However, they probably do have a greater number of significant secondary influences on human affairs than any other pattern or complex of patterns.

Action: Making Decisions

In the 1970s and 80s, the American view of Japanese corporations went something like this: Japanese prices were lower because wages in Japan were lower. Their products were good because their plants and equipment were newer. They received all kinds of hidden support from the Japanese government, and they didn't abide by the rules of fair trade.

To those who looked more closely at reasons for the phenomenal improvement in the quality of Japanese manufactures during this era, these explanations weren't adequate. Far more important, most of them said, was the Japanese style of management. They pointed to American companies within the United States that had been taken over by the Japanese and with the same employees, paid the same wages, using the same plant and equipment, were able to markedly increase production, improve quality, and decrease employee turnover and absenteeism.

The heart of the Japanese approach to management, those who studied the matter said, was decision making by consensus. A very flat organizational structure was used; everyone involved in the organization communicated with everyone else; and nothing was done until everyone had an opportunity to contribute suggestions, understand the whole matter, and agree that a particular policy, procedure, or product was the most desirable. This approach contrasted with traditional American approaches to management, in which decisions were made at the top and imposed on those below.

The contrast in performance of most corporations that practice consensus decision making and those that don't provides evidence that patterns for decision making in industry have far-reaching consequences. That the same proposition applies elsewhere—in politics, in education, in religious and civic organizations, in the military, in the family—should be apparent. The relevance stems in large part, no doubt, from the fact that in many societies the drive for some kind of personal autonomy is very strong. Most individuals seem to want to participate in the making of decisions that affect them, and therefore react negatively or positively to particular patterns for decision making depending on the extent of their participation in the process.

It's interesting and sometimes helpful to know that in many societies there's considerable consistency in all major patterns related to decision making. Authoritarian or participative patterns for making decisions in religious matters are often paralleled by acceptance of similar patterns in politics, education, industry, and the family. In other societies this consistency is absent and subtle psychological stresses often result.

Other Patterns of Action

In addition to the action patterns just identified, an overview of the important patterns of action for societies and systems ought to include several others. Patterns for ownership, for recruiting or replacing members, playing, displaying status, communicating, social service, defense, special days, worship, keeping insiders in and outsiders out, mobility, caring for the self, and for expressing creativity, need to be known, as well as other patterns that might become apparent when one is attempting to make sense of particular groups. In some societies, for example, patterns for manipulating the spirit world or nature through supernatural means are important.

In every case, however, shared patterns of action—the usual and typical ways the members of a system behave—are central to sense making.

SHARED IDEAS

The phrase "shared ideas" carries a great deal of weight, standing in for "worldview," "cultural assumptions," "values and beliefs," "cognitive system," "cognitive configuration," and other words and phrases having to do with shared states of mind. Every society or social system has a body of shared ideas that function as a kind of glue holding it together. These ideas are almost always so deeply imbedded and so taken for granted that most within the system aren't aware of them. If the ideas are pointed out, members will tend to think that, rather than being peculiar to their own group, the ideas are products of "human nature" shared by all "normal" human beings everywhere. The basic difficulty they're having is suggested by that old, loaded-with-meaning saying, "A fish would be the last to discover water."

One of several components of every society's body of shared ideas is its time orientation. Middle-class Americans, for example, tend to be future oriented. They spend large amounts of time and money on education

Figure 2.12.

(and have a relatively low school drop-out rates) because they believe that sometime in the future this behavior will pay off. They put money in savings accounts to buy future pleasure. They invest, confident that, though the stock market may be in a slump, if they're patient enough the investment will eventually be profitable. Starting early, they tend to live in a state of anticipation ("Just wait until I get my driver's license … a car of my own … an apartment … married … a house on Riverside Drive … a divorce … Just wait …").

The middle classes of other societies also tend to be future oriented, but most of the world's population isn't. Some are present oriented, some past oriented, and others oriented toward life after death. To each society, the actions of other societies or sub-societies with different time orientations will either be incomprehensible or may seem unrealistic, irresponsible, or downright immoral.

Every society has a dozen or so fundamental, unexamined shared ideas that structure most of the actions of most of its members. What's considered the "best" time—past, present, future, or the hereafter—is only one. Shared ideas about the nature of nature, beliefs about the causes of events and change, images of the good life, conceptions of the self, and ideas about the characteristics and role of the supernatural are others. Information about a society's unexamined assumptions is the most useful information that can be known about it, more important by far than facts about its economic system, its natural resources, geography, social structure, or history. But shared states of mind are also the hardest to understand, partly because, as noted earlier, it's so difficult to take the first step—to realize that we ourselves have a distinctive way of looking at the world, seeing it not as it actually is but modeling it as the society into which we were socialized models it.

The members of a system may not be aware of the main ideas shaping their lives, but those ideas determine nearly everything they do. Within each system, the movements of dancers, the appearance and arrangement of buildings for work and worship, the holidays anticipated, the traits of those admired, the content of textbooks, the nature and distribution of tools, the flow of musical compositions, the views from doors and windows—these and almost everything else of consequence grow out of the rarely examined shared ideas of members. They're the most important thing that can be known about ourselves and each other and yet, incredibly, their study isn't in the traditional curriculum. It's not even being *discussed* as a study that ought to be in the curriculum.

A comprehensive analysis of the many dimensions of each society's shared ideas is too much to undertake here, but a brief review of several should serve to emphasize their importance in making sense of our own individual and collective behavior and that of others. Of particular usefulness is an understanding of ideas that grow out of what might be called "unavoidable aspects of experience." The earth, its major features, others, time, cause and effect—these and a few other aspects of experience are so much a part of life, every society will have devised a body of ideas about them.

Shared Ideas: The Self

The self is one such unavoidable aspect of experience. Every individual is faced by the fact of self—can look down and see the physical self or view its reflection in a pond or mirror. Around awareness of self the members of each society build a cluster of ideas. These tend to be considered products of insight into the true nature of the self, but it would be more accurate to describe them as inventions or myths, products less of insight than of experience-triggered imagination.

People, understandably, are enormously interested in the self even in societies in which self-effacement is important, but few are aware of most of the ideas about the self they've acquired from their native society, ideas used constantly as guides to action, attitude, and feeling.

One of those important ideas can be clarified by looking at what might be called "boundaries of the self" in various societies. Consider, for example, the fact that members of a single nuclear American family—parents and grown children—may be scattered across America or even abroad.

Their earned incomes may vary, sometimes greatly, a fact that isn't ordinarily considered unfair. Each member is expected, under normal circumstances, to be self-sufficient, to carry insurance or make some other provision to cover loss.

The members of many other societies consider these American practices not only strange but unacceptable. To be cut off from one's family or clan for long periods of time would, they feel, deprive one of one's principal source of happiness—would, in fact, make life hardly worth living. Neither could any honorable reason be advanced to explain why members of the very same family would choose not to share incomes so each could live as well as the others. And finally, to go to strangers if one is sick or in need of money would be unthinkable—an affront to one's family and a threat to an arrangement that, if necessary, provides dependable, concerned care.

Two differing conceptions of the nature of the self help explain these very different practices. A metaphor may clarify: Individual Americans tend to be "marbles"; individuals in some other societies are "fingers on a hand." Marbles may be held together, but even when they're squeezed tightly in a "family," they remain separate and distinct. Size, color, and configuration (identity) remain unchanged by the closeness. And if the hand is opened, the marbles roll off in different directions, still unchanged.

But fingers are different. If one is a "finger," one is an organic part of something else, something larger and more important. There's a sense of distinctiveness (no two fingers are alike) but not of separateness. One functions most effectively in harmony with others, in fact *can* only function effectively *with* the rest of the family. The welfare of each is bound up in the welfare of the whole. To be cut off, to have no close, working relationship with the family, deprives one of the most fundamental reason for existence. One might as well be dead and, in a few groups, death appears to actually result from separation. The individual continues to eat, continues to drink, continues to maintain physical care of the body, but dies nevertheless.

A discussion of the self as marble or finger barely begins an exploration of the concept. In some societies, conceptions of the self are inextricably linked to dead ancestors and unborn descendants; in others, to the political state. In some, the use of phrases such as "a child of God" or "at one with the Spirit" suggest still other perceptions of the boundaries of the self.

Different answers to the question, "What are the boundaries of the self?" help explain differences in behavior from society to society. Other questions related to the self are equally important. Are individuals within the system of equal or of varying worth? Is perceived worth a constant, bestowed at birth and continuing in full until death, or does it vary with age, sex, birth order, family? Is the self inherently good, inherently bad, or "neutral"? What are the rhythms, stages, cycles, or states of the self? What's its structure? For example, Americans tend toward a fragmented conception of the self, the self as several selves—physical, mental, emotional, spiritual—each self rather autonomous, while in other societies the self is seen as housing two warring entities or is one integrated whole.

In every society or system a range of ideas having to do with the nature and identity of the self have evolved and are shared, giving a distinctive character to the economic, political, social, esthetic, and religious activity within the system.

Shared Ideas: Significant Others

"Sixty-Three Killed in Plane Crash," says the newspaper headline. The reader brings the paper closer. Eyes move from line to line down the page. When the sentence, "No Americans were reported aboard," is reached, many Americans move to a different news item.

All humans look out from the vantage point of the self and see others. For any number of reasons, including dependency, proximity, instruction, and experience, "others" tend to be viewed as having varying degrees of significance. If one visualizes a series of concentric circles with the self (usually, but not always) occupying the innermost circle, significant others are those who occupy the other circles, their relative significance represented by their distance from the self. How much of the news story is read depends largely upon the positions of others on this circle. If reading stops when identity has been established, one must assume that those killed weren't particularly significant to the reader. Indeed, the very fact that some version of the sentence appears at all suggests that, to the writer as well as the reader, the world is divided into individuals and peoples of varying significance.

The criteria for ranking others according to degree of significance are often affection, honor, or respect. Perhaps the most useful approach to identifying shared ideas about relative significance is to rank others on the basis of the amount of activity attributable to a relationship and the intensity of feeling which accompanies the activity. For example, for most Americans, neighbors were once very significant others. This often isn't true today.

Every individual's significant others will of course differ, but in every society certain tendencies will be apparent. In some, parents will rank next to or even above the self. In other systems, religious leaders will be very significant. Grandparents and other family members will be considered more or less significant depending upon the group. American kids reared within the dominant culture, asked to draw those concentric circles and locate their significant others within them, will often not even mention grandparents. In other societies, even rather distant relatives will rank above friends. In some groups, workmates are particularly significant. In others, they count for little unless they're also friends.

The concentric circles can be usefully extended to include large categories of people. Nationalities, races, ethnic groups, or those with certain religious affiliations, for example, can be ranked according to degree of perceived significance. Because each category of significant other carries with it expectations, obligations, responsibilities, and attitudes that prompt certain ways of acting, making sense of the ways of acting within a system requires an awareness of who counts for how much.

Shared Ideas: Causation

The sun comes up. The baby gets sick. A war breaks out. Flowers bloom. A lost key is found. It rains. The cathedral catches fire. A bus skids on the wet pavement. A tiger attacks at the watering hole. The cancer disappears. The potatoes rot in the ground. Money comes unexpectedly in the mail. The volcano erupts. The snow is dry. The leak stops.

Why? No one knows for certain, but the members of every society think they know, think they can explain, at least in general terms, the causes of most consequences. They also think that the explanations they advance are so obviously true, so logical, so objectively verifiable, so far beyond question, that discussion of them is almost pointless. Further, they believe that other explanations of why things happen are so absurd, so illogical, so demonstrably false they could only be a product of naiveté, superstition, ignorance, or perversity.

Why does it rain? It rains because atmospheric conditions are conducive to rain. It rains because, in God's Grand Design, each rain is preordained. It rains because, through the rain, an omnipotent God can manipulate the beliefs and attitudes of humans. It rains because the rain ritual has been performed so precisely there's no alternative. It rains because the Spirit of the Rain wills it. It rains in response to prayer. There are dozens, perhaps hundreds of "reasons" why it rains. In every group, one or two explanations are believed implicitly. The rest won't be considered worth taking seriously.

Why does the stomach ache? It aches because of a chemical imbalance. It aches because the mouth was open in the presence of those who cause evil spirits to enter. It aches in order to punish. It aches because a pin has been inserted in a voodoo doll. It aches because Fate wills it.

A considerable variety of assumptions about causation are held by sub-groups or societies within the United States. The dominant society tends to put great store in two principal explanations. Things happen because of the operation of chemical and physical forces, and things happen because humans make them happen. The operation of chemical and physical forces explains rain, volcanic eruptions, stomach aches, television, sunsets, and hardening of the arteries. People are responsible for wars, traffic accidents, fund drives, hospitals, concerts, murder, taxes, and poverty.

School textbooks teach these two "primary causes"; the media reinforce their centrality, and common sense and science are cited in support of their validity. Effects that are different or impossible to trace to one of these causes are generally ignored or attributed to trickery. Those who show interest in other possible causes are viewed with suspicion and, if the interested party is engaged in research, funds are usually very hard or impossible to obtain.

Shared Ideas: Space

Human systems exist in physical space. Over long periods of time, various attitudes and assumptions about this space evolve and begin to shape how people act. As with all components of a society's shared ideas, however, neither the distinctiveness of these ideas nor their implications are ordinarily recognized by those who share them.

One of the more familiar illustrations of this fact has to do with the idea of personal space—the "bubble" extending outward from the surface of the body that's felt to be one's private domain. It's surprising how few individuals have attempted to trace the outlines of their own personal space or have given thought to variations in it related to particular others. Nor are many aware of differences from group to group in the size and shape of personal space and the reactions to various kinds of perceived violations of it.

Personal space is one space-related component of a society's shared ideas, and perhaps not a very important one. It can be a source of irritation and misunderstanding, and it may occasionally contribute to small-scale problems, but the fact that a group's ideas about the proper dimensions of personal space can apparently change without altering other ideas or ways of acting, suggests that it's usually not very significant.

Other space-related concepts, however, have really important behavioral consequences. Traditionally, Bolivian tin miners showed respect for an underworld figure they called "Tio" when they went underground. Tio, or Satan, was considered preeminent in the space below ground level, as

Christ was preeminent in the space above. Between the U.S. Army Corps of Engineers and various Native American tribes there's a long history of conflict traceable to differing assumptions about certain spaces. In ancient Israel, that portion of the temple called the "Holy of Holies" was related to differently than other space. Sacred groves, burial grounds, altars, haunted houses, and the locations of supernatural manifestations or important historical events are also often treated differently, and almost always require changes in behavior when one is at or near them, such as removing a hat or lowering the voice. Even feelings about the relative desirability of residing in the bush, on the mountain, at the seashore, or "beyond the sound of another man's axe" are space-related ideas that help explain ways of acting.

Shared Ideas: Ownership

It's Christmas morning before dawn. The children, just awake, run downstairs and into the living room. Unopened packages pyramid under the tree and spill out across the carpet. Catching the light is a new bicycle. A tag hangs from the handlebars. "Merry Christmas," it says, "from Mom and Dad to All You Kids."

It's not hard to imagine what would be likely to happen next. American children, like their parents, tend to assign ownership of the various parts of the material world to individuals, and are ill-prepared for most alternatives. Bicycles, and just about everything else, are supposed to belong to some *one*.

From the assumption that bicycles, automobiles, houses, farmland, forests, mountains, and minerals (and decisions about their use) should be in the hands of individuals, much follows. From the assumption that almost everything is owned jointly by all members of a society, different actions follow. From the belief that entities called "corporations" can be created which, like individuals, can own and control but, unlike individuals, can live indefinitely, yet another cluster of effects follows.

Who can own? Only males? Children? Spirits? Those of a particular religious affiliation? What kinds of things can be owned? Personal effects only? Land? Water? Symbols? Other humans? How extensive are the rights and privileges which accompany ownership? Can one do anything one wants with what one owns, including destroy it? Is ownership transferable? Held in trust? What special responsibilities or obligations, if any, accompany ownership?

Beliefs and assumptions about ownership send out tentacles that reach into the remotest parts of societies, affecting how individuals act, how family members relate, and how institutions and nations function.

Shared Ideas: The Good Life

The members of every society share some kind of mental image of the most desirable style of life. This image of "the good life" helps explain much human action—everything from the kind of education parents afford their kids to the nature of the most common kinds of criminal activity. In evaluating an educational system, most parents really want to know if it will enable their children not so much to be educated as to achieve the good life. The thief is pursuing the same objective, just using a different strategy.

The struggle for the good life manifests itself in innumerable ways. The 1920s political slogan, "Two chickens in every pot," presented an image of the good life. The heading "Be Your Own Boss" in boldface type in the classified section of the newspaper is an attempt to use conceptions of the good life to attract attention. The advertising photographer who fills his backgrounds with out-of-focus but discernable symbols of the good life hopes those symbols will be subconsciously noted and attached to the product being promoted, even if the two aren't logically related.

"The Good Life" as a title for a category of ideas to study is a rather large umbrella for several ideas that provide insight into the nature of human societies. Most Americans, for example, think it's human nature to want to "move up" in life. They have a hard time believing that, in some societies, people would feel threatened by the possibility of upward social mobility. For some of the world's population, however, that's the case. More fearful about the possibility of falling down the status ladder than attracted by the benefits of climbing up, they prefer a rigid arrangement guaranteeing a position even if that position is low.

Since most conceptions of the good life are easily translated into value terms, one of the most direct ways to summarize a group's image of the good life is with statements such as, "It's good to move up," or, "It's good to know your place." Here are several additional statements drawn from various societies that reflect conceptions of certain elements of the good life:

It's good to be young, beautiful, and active.
It's good to have many male children.
It's good to own lots of things.
It's good to be old and respected.
It's good to win.
It's good to avoid satisfying physiological desires.
It's good to be dependent.

It's good to hide one's true feelings.

It's good to be indistinguishable from others.

It's good to be clean.

It's good to be part of a network bound together by obligations.

Because ideas about the good life are usually the most familiar component of a group's system of thought, they're sometimes questioned or subjected to rational analysis. It isn't unusual for example, to hear an American say, "Well, money isn't everything," or "Beauty is only skin deep." However, the power of early socialization isn't easy to push away.

Those not aware of their society's conceptions of the good life are prisoners of those conceptions. They can't choose to accept or reject ideas for which they can't imagine alternatives. Common sense and everyday experience don't provide either a clear picture of one's own images of the good life or of possible alternatives.

Other Shared States of Mind

In addition to the shared ideas just identified, all societies hold other important ones—ideas about the nature of nature, about other societies, about trends and directions of change, about their own action patterns, about the meaning of existence, and about the supernatural. And, as was noted earlier, assumptions about time also explain much human behavior. Some societies (but perhaps not middle-class Americans) have very strongly held ideas about an individual's relationship with and responsibilities to the larger society, ideas that manifest themselves in differing attitudes toward taxes and social service.

No really satisfactory category system for shared ideas has as yet been devised. The categories used here aren't discrete; the same information could be categorized in a variety of ways, and important ideas shaping behavior have probably been overlooked. But if sense is to be made of experience, a start must be made, and crude tools are better than none. Nothing we can know about ourselves is more important than why we do what we do, so cognitive systems must be studied. "Studied" doesn't mean making them the focus of a week or so of work or even a year-long class. It means that year after year, in subject after subject, what's taught is deliberately related to the states of mind that shape human societies and determine their historical trajectories.

Figure 2.13.

SYSTEMIC RELATIONSHIPS

An old Chinese riddle asks: If you have a horse and cart, how many things do you have? The answer? Three. A horse, a cart, and a horse and cart.

Organized human groups—civilizations, societies, social systems—are the makers or inventors of "sense." Four distinct kinds of information about them have been described in detail: information about the places they occupy, the actors composing them, the actors' customary ways of acting, and important ideas they share. Time is the fifth dimension, which becomes important when investigating change. But the five are six. Their relationships generate a sixth kind of information.

To use the Model to describe and analyze environment, actors, action, and shared ideas, reality must be made to "stand still," frozen in time while the environment is inventoried, the actors counted, their typical actions described, and the probable reasons for those actions identified.

But of course societies never stand still. They're constantly evolving and changing, sometimes rapidly, sometimes almost imperceptibly, but changing nevertheless. Environment, actors, action, and shared ideas are constantly interacting over time, and those interactions create a whole greater than the sum of the parts. If sense is to be made, that whole must be understood. In the distinctive drama unfolding in every society, each of the four has a reality of its own, but how the play turns out depends on their interactions.

Before discussing the use of the Model in the study of relationships, it's helpful to remember that the discovery of relationships is the second step of the basic process by means of which human knowledge is expanded. The first is the discernment of patterns—reaction patterns, growth patterns, behavior patterns, patterns on an oscilloscope, patterns of symptoms, patterns of response—any and all patterns. When we say we understand something, we usually mean we see a pattern, then link that pattern to something else—temperature, anxiety, diet, political persuasion, impurities in the mix, childhood trauma, altitude, planetary motion, trust, corrosion, overcrowding, whatever.

As has been said repeatedly, maximizing opportunities to explore relationships requires that everything known be part of a single, integrated, mutually supportive framework of knowledge. The Model provides that framework, and the traditional disciplines don't. They use different vocabularies, different investigation techniques, create different conceptual frameworks, function at different levels of abstraction. The Model, on the other hand, is comprehensive, so when learners focus attention on something about which they know little or nothing, it allows them to sweep their minds across everything they know, unobstructed by artificial or arbitrary boundaries, in a search for anything or everything that might relate.

Imagine, for example, giving two matched classes of adolescents an important but ridiculously difficult, open-ended, year-end assignment, one class having spent the year studying world history, the other having spent the year constructing the Model. The assignment asks for explanations involving relationships:

> At various times in human history, one nation or another has accumulated vast wealth and power and dominated the world. Egypt and Greece were early examples, more recently, Spain and England. During the 20th Century, America held that position. How many possible explanations of why empires disintegrate or fall can you think of?

It's reasonable to suppose that the class that spent the year studying world history would try to lift answers primarily from what they'd read in the textbook and heard the teacher say.

Their effort would be of limited success. The assignment asks for generalizations, and openly stated generalizations, hypotheses, conclusions, and so on, being matters of opinion, aren't really acceptable in history textbooks. Textbook selection committees are looking for facts, not opinions. Authors slip them in, but a conscientious textbook selection committee will find them, and if the generalizations aren't currently politically correct, the book won't be adopted.

The class would, then, have to generalize from the facts available, and would probably conclude that economic problems or political instability, or both, weakened empires sufficiently to allow hostile neighbors to defeat them and take control. The class would probably formulate four or five hypotheses positing that empires fell as balances of power changed. All answers, of course, would be based on recall of secondhand information.

Given the above assignment, would the class that spent the year elaborating the Model protest, complaining that the assignment wasn't fair because they hadn't studied world history?

No. They'd have learned in the course of the year how to use the Model as an analytical *tool*, and would just assume that this final assignment, like all previous assignments, was asking them to demonstrate their ability to *use* that tool. They'd know that something—probably something very complicated—had happened to Egypt, Greece, Spain and England, and they were being asked to bring the analytical tool they'd developed to bear on that "something," speculating about what it might have been.

What they'd take to the assignment is some version of the elaboration of the Model found in Figure 2.14.

A first reaction to this elaboration may be that it's long and complex. Should this be the case, keep in mind that the framework:

- Is far shorter than a comparable listing of the major concepts of the "core" curriculum
- Uses only already known and familiar categories, subcategories, and so on
- Is free of jargon
- Is in constant use, even by small children
- Is universal, applicable to the description and analyses of any reality, any time, any place.

Keep in mind also that the conceptual framework isn't something abruptly imposed on learners with the expectation that it be memorized. It's eventually "owned" by them because, properly introduced, it's been constructed and elaborated over time by learners themselves as they attempt to make better sense of concrete, real-world experience.

The Model says to think about everything systemically. Empires are systems, and systems have "moving parts." They occupy an environment with certain resources, use certain tools, enjoy or endure certain climates, are protected from enemies by mountains or water, or are exposed to them by plains. They have wealth in various forms, and symbol systems that either do or don't allow them to design complex structures, weapons, and means for communicating. Did anything about "Environment"

A comprehensive, supradisciplinary, systemically-integrated organizer of general knowledge.

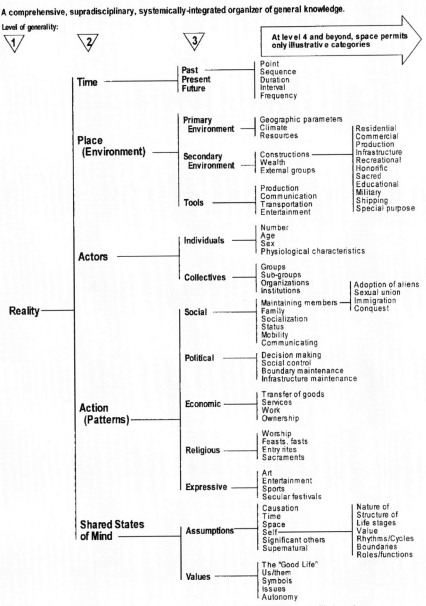

Figure 2.14.

change over time? If so, how? With what possible consequences for the empire?

If, for example, it's known that wood was a major energy source for ancient Rome, and that over the centuries it became increasingly scarce and costly to obtain; that fact can be treated as a given and every other component of the model "checked out" to identify significant relationships. Any other category is simply chosen and hypotheses about a possible relationship generated. Did the energy situation affect demographics—the distribution and density of members, for example? Did it alter environment—its size through territorial acquisition? Its use? Other resources? The design of structures? Technology? Did the energy situation affect patterns for work? For status? Family organization? Making decisions? For distributing wealth? Did changes in the availability of energy alter in any way Roman conceptions of the good life? Ideas about significant others? Self? Their time orientation?

The same procedure can be followed with all components of the Model. If, for example, one knows with some certainty that in ancient Rome's later years the income gap between rich and poor tended to widen, every other component of the Model is available as a source of possible explanatory hypotheses.

It really makes little difference now what Rome's energy problems may have been, or how wide the range of citizens' incomes. But once it's been demonstrated that demographics, environment, patterns of action, and the shared states of mind of a society are systemically related, and that the sources, characteristics, and availability of energy do indeed affect human societies in any number of significant ways, the resultant complex of Model-generated concepts can be applied to societies that *are* important—one's own and those with which one must coexist. Incidentally, it shouldn't take more than a few minutes of this kind of play with the Model to see just how arbitrary and limiting the traditional disciplines can be. The search for useful relationships may lead anywhere. To channel students into courses and programs that erect artificial boundaries between aspects of reality does them a real and permanent disservice.

System Change

It's the easiest of steps from a study of relationships to a study of the dynamics of change within societies or systems. A relationship statement reads "A relates to B." To begin an exploration of change, the statement is simply extended to "A change in A will probably change B, and vice versa."

Sense making requires an understanding of the dynamics of change, and a foundation for that understanding should begin to be built in the earliest years of education. That social change, so related to everyday life, so omnipresent, so powerful, so much a factor in the effort to survive and achieve individual and collective stability and happiness, is almost entirely ignored by the traditional curriculum, is unacceptable. Adolescents are capable of making sufficient sense of the dynamics of change to analyze it, give thought to the stresses and problems it creates, and devise policies and strategies for skirting the problems and alleviating the stresses. That they're sent into a complex, increasingly dangerous future without those skills is inexcusable.

System Change: Static Tendencies

Dirty looks, burning books, ridicule, prison, banishment, head shaving, asylums, ostracism, hanging, the threat of Hell—in all societies the weapons devised for use against those who appear to threaten the status quo are numerous, varied, and often ingenious.

In Roman-occupied territory, those who threatened the established order were sometimes crucified. Among the Amish, an individual who fails to conform to accepted practices may be shunned, going for months or years without being spoken to by family or friends. In parts of southern India, a man who "looks at young and beautiful girls and describes their dresses and shapes" is told to expect in the afterlife to be "nailed to the wall with sharp nails and then thrown into melting limestone and have limewater thrown into his eyes." History books contain myriad accounts of individuals who met untimely ends because they appeared to threaten established ways of acting or questioned their society's shared ideas. About mid-20th century, many school boards across the United States spent hours trying to decide what to do about male students who came to school without belts in their trousers, or with hair falling below their collars.

All societies have two treasures, threats to which are almost certain to bring defensive measures swinging into action. One of these treasures is its standard ways of acting—the accepted way of organizing families, distributing wealth, associating, and other action patterns discussed earlier. The other treasure is their shared ideas.

The two treasures have guardians: the Elders, the Klan, the Village Council, the Censor, the Citizens for a Safer Athens, the John Birch Society, the Un-American Activities Committee. In every society, in every era, the ultimate threat is "the threat to our way of life." "Our way of life" means "our ways of acting, and the main ideas we share."

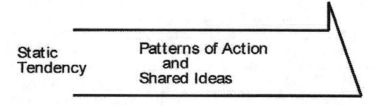

Figure 2.15.

Despite determined efforts to keep them unchanged, a system's ways of acting and its shared ideas are never completely static. They evolve, and are sometimes deliberately changed to make them more consistent with each other, as when racial patterns in America's schools were changed in the 1950s to more closely align them with an American assumption that "all people are created equal." But the evolution is usually slow, the change reluctant. Very little change occurs within social systems because members desire it. What may at first appear to be a deliberate move in a new direction is more likely, when studied closely, to be a mere course correction designed to restore, insulate, or maintain prevailing ways of acting and thinking, both of which are powerfully inclined to be static.

System Change: Dynamic Tendencies

Societies don't ordinarily change because those within them are unhappy with their ideas and ways of acting and deliberately set out to alter them. Nevertheless, ideas and ways of acting do change, often very rapidly, and in directions that are often not to the liking of those within the system.

One might assume that changes that come about despite their general unpopularity must surely be imposed by outsiders, that a powerful elite or a militarily superior neighbor is responsible. That's generally not the case. In fact, direct threats often result not in change but in an increased attachment to traditional ways of acting and thinking. As many conquerors have discovered, physical force is a very poor tool for bringing about desired social change. Shielded by doors or codes, traditional ways may defy forceful change for decades or centuries.

Then what *does* cause change when it isn't desired? Why is it that, despite deliberate resistance, ways of acting and shared ideas change nevertheless? The answer lies primarily in characteristics inherent in the actors and environment components of the Model. The natural tendency

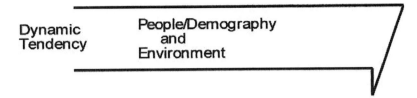

Figure 2.16.

of ways of acting and thinking is to be static, but actor and environment characteristics tend to be dynamic, unstable, even uncontrollable.

And since societies are true systems, the inevitable and uncontrollable changes within actors and environment alter actions and shared ideas despite determined, often organized resistance.

The instability of actor and environmental characteristics is inherent. For example, there's no acceptable way for the members of most societies to achieve and maintain absolutely zero population growth. Population is therefore always increasing or decreasing, and either trend triggers other changes throughout the system. Some societies have so geared their institutions to population growth that zero growth itself creates change.

The number of members of a system can't be rigidly controlled, and neither can the relative size of various age groupings, the balance of males to females, the climate, the available resources, the reshaping of the earth by nature, or any aspect or characteristic of actors and environment. Even within highly totalitarian societies controlled by leaders who understand the destabilizing effects of change and try to "freeze" various change factors, major change is inevitable. Rigid enforcement of a pass system to control citizen movement may briefly maintain existing population distribution patterns, or a particular technological innovation may be destroyed or outlawed, but no strategy works for long.

And even if some way is devised to arrest one or two change factors, some are simply beyond human regulation. When a long-term weather cycle that's brought adequate rain to an area for many years comes to an end, there's going to be social change, and nothing can be done to stop it. Alternative sources of water may be found, but the very process of switching to those alternatives will create change. The use of irreplaceable resources has the same effect. When an oil field has been pumped dry, it's dry. The earth has one less oil field forever. The change is irreversible. Soon or late, the consequences are going to ripple through those human systems that have anything either directly or indirectly to do with oil.

Changes in actors and environments are inevitable. And, because a society's ways of acting and its shared ideas have usually grown out of, and

are therefore related to, those characteristics, they can't remain unaffected. If patterns for work are based on the supply of fish in the river and
the fish disappear, the old pattern must either be abandoned or become
ritual. Either way, the pattern for work has changed. If ideas about "the
good life" are based on an economy of abundance, and exhaustion of
resources dictates an economy of scarcity, old ideas about the good life
will either change or those who hold them will be miserable or considered
mentally ill.

The second reason why changes within actors and environment have
such tremendous power to trigger other changes is that they generally
occur below the threshold of awareness of most members of the society
affected. Few social systems have either the means to measure or an interest in precisely measuring happenings within each of the Model's components. Americans, for example, pay a great deal of attention to events that
unfold more or less instantaneously—the hijacking, the court decision,
the exposure of an instance of corruption, the eruption of a volcano. But
cumulative events—those made up of myriad small actions or instances
stretching over long intervals of time, generally receive little or no attention. An oil spill with a temporarily adverse effect on a body of water will
almost always draw the helicopters of the news services. But when individual drops of oil from automobile engine crankcases and transmissions collect on the surface of parking lots, then wash into storm sewers and do
equal or greater damage to the same body of water, it won't even make the
back pages of newspapers.

Changes in actors and environment tend to be all but invisible. The
medical researcher whose work will lengthen life expectancy by several
weeks isn't trying to subvert the social security system, create another Sun
City in Florida, or increase the political power of senior citizens. Alone in
the laboratory, the researcher is simply trying to solve a problem, meet a
challenge, earn a salary, and maybe a laudatory article in a medical journal. The cascading consequences of the work being done—the changes in
neighborhoods, in taxes, in medical costs, and in much else—will be
below most citizens' level of awareness.

Individual decisions to have a child, move to another place, drill a
water well, buy a wood-burning space heater, pay a small bribe, or travel
abroad, make no headlines and attract no particular notice, but when
those kinds of action are replicated thousands or millions of times, the
effect is almost always far more significant than are most of the events that
actually make headlines. Cumulative events are often ignored until the
river is completely dead, the economy is foundering, the faucets run dry,
or the desert reaches subdivisions. When the situation is finally noted,
social changes to adequately cope with the resultant problems may create

so much stress, cost so much, or generate so many new problems, the society can't afford to address them.

There's nothing particularly complex or mysterious about the basic processes of social change. Most upper-elementary-aged children can take each of the components of actors and environment and point out at least some of the pressures that changes in them exert on other aspects of the whole system. Unfortunately, American society (perhaps because the schools have little or nothing to say on the subject and thereby imply that it's not important) functions on the basis of considerably simpler conceptions of the dynamics of change.

There was for a time an appreciation of the system-disturbing power of technological innovation. It led to the creation in 1972 of a Congressional advisory committee called the Office of Technological Assessment, but it was closed in 1995, in response to Republican Party criticism that it was unnecessary. During its twenty-four-year life it produced about 750 studies on a wide range of topics, including acid rain, health care, global climate change, and polygraphs. That the OTA was shut down with so little fanfare is further evidence of the traditional curriculum's failure to produce a citizenry aware of the dynamics of change and the problems change generates.

Technology is recognized by most Americans as a trigger of change, but more deeply embedded in the public mind is the assumption that things change mostly because of the actions of people. This assumption, in part no doubt a legacy of an earlier time when those in power commissioned the only written record of events, is reinforced by most American history textbooks, and by mainstream media. Things happen, according to this view, because they were made to happen by Hitler, Congress, the Founding Fathers, King George III, the President, liberals, conservatives, Osama Ben Laden, or some other individual or group.

There's another, less tangible assumption about social change that can be found in some societies or segments of society—a generalized feeling that what happens isn't the result of complex (but understandable) factors but is instead a product of forces or plans of other than earthly origin. There's no way, of course, to know whether or not this belief is valid, but to the extent that it's accepted, it makes other possible explanations of social change irrelevant and an understanding of them unnecessary. Those who subscribe to this view perceive social change primarily in moral terms. Collective success or failure, growth or decline, survival or extinction, is thought to hinge primarily on responses to moral questions. "Good" societies flourish; "bad" ones are punished and die.

If this isn't the whole story, and earthly factors do indeed play an important role in social change, then each of the subcategories and sub-

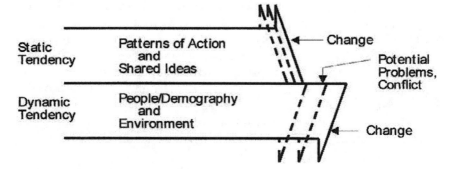

Figure 2.17.

subcategories of actors and environment in the Model needs to be understood and its relationship to other categories monitored.

System Integration

Societies being systems, their four main parts interact over time. Environment, Actors, Actions, and Shared Ideas fit together and are usually mutually supportive. In the United States, for example, conceptions of the self as a separate, independent entity without organic ties to an extended family or clan mesh with patterns for work and the distribution of wealth. Since free enterprise requires a very mobile labor supply—individuals willing and able to move quickly and easily from one place to another—middle-class American ideas about the self fit well with the demands of work patterns.

However, primarily because of factors related to social change, various aspects of societies often *don't* integrate smoothly, and stress of one kind or another results. For example, middle-class Americans place a high value on autonomy, on "freedom," on being one's "own boss." Consistent with this assumption of what's good are several ways of acting, including those for making decisions. In the political realm, there's democracy and the vote. In religion, there are many denominations, widespread use of congregational forms of governance, and the option not to be religious at all. In many families, there's discussion and shared decision making—ways of acting consistent with broadly shared American ideas.

But in other areas of American life, ways of acting aren't consistent with shared beliefs. Assumptions about the self often aren't consistent with the patterns for decision making common in American industry, in education, and in other institutions. Workplace and school organization often hark back to military models—authoritarian and hierarchical—with little provision for shared decision making. As a consequence, for many Americans, work really is *work*, and school is akin to a medium-security prison. Deep-seated negative feelings about work and school aren't just routinely obvious but are verified by studies that indicate elevated levels of stress with physical and psychological costs. On the other hand, organizations and industries that do try to accommodate societal values, that flatten organizational hierarchy, minimize status differences in facilities, and establish procedures for open communication, are generally happier, more productive, and profitable. If they don't work, it's usually because they don't synchronize well with other system components stuck in old patterns.

The degree of integration of the various components of social systems changes constantly, but generally speaking, actor and environment pressures tend to push system components apart, while efforts related to action and shared ideas tend to push them toward alignment. It's a complicated picture, but the Model helps organize the study of internal consistencies and inconsistencies by identifying relevant parts of the system and allowing them to be easily juxtaposed so learners can identify problems and sources of stress not yet part of general public consciousness. Adolescents ordinarily have no problem making sense of the forces and counter-forces to which societies subject themselves.

NOTE

1. Reprinted with permission of John Perry.

PART THREE

THE MODEL AND THE TRADITIONAL CURRICULUM

It goes without saying that no two students are alike. Each comes to formal instruction with a complex mix of interests, abilities, life experiences, goals, values, prior knowledge, and future prospects likely to be affected at least in part by many factors, including social class, family background, friends, place of residence, physical appearance, personality, wealth, and luck.

It also goes without saying that the learner's future is unknown and unknowable, making it impossible to identify the particular knowledge most likely to eventually prove valuable.

Given all these variables, the whole idea of required, specialized studies seems counterproductive, particularly when those requirements weren't the product of an extended public debate or scholarly dialog, but were instead merely the work of the Committee of Ten. The "core curriculum" they recommended—a random mix of math, science, language arts, and social studies courses—is now so taken for granted, so deeply embedded in the public mind and in bureaucracy, that any significant change seems unlikely.

There's an old story that illustrates the present situation and the problem.

The boiler tender at a factory in a small town was in charge of blowing the noon whistle signaling workers to break for lunch.

What's Worth Learning?
pp. 71–88
Copyright © 2011 by Information Age Publishing

He took his job seriously, faithfully checking his watch every morning as he walked past the clock on a pole in front of the jewelry store on Main Street.

One Saturday afternoon, suddenly curious, he stopped in to see the jeweler.

"I've been wondering," he said, "how you keep your clock on exactly the right time."

"Easy," said the jeweler. "I set it every day when the noon whistle blows."

In America's schools, subject-matter standardized tests in the four "core" areas of the curriculum are keyed to subject-matter standards, and those standards are keyed to the tests. It's an incestuous, self-reinforcing cycle repeating itself decade after decade, impervious to social change and the needs of learners, unaffected by the knowledge explosion and new insights into the nature of learning, and unmindful of mountains of research and common sense that says machine-scored standardized tests can't measure and attach meaningful numbers to complex thought processes.

Keying tests to standards keyed to a curriculum adopted in 1893 is an invitation to institutional and societal disaster. One would think that more than a century of failed attempts to maintain a system for educating that treats human variability as a problem rather than as an evolutionary triumph would lead to a fundamental reevaluation of the curriculum, but that hasn't happened. If an alternative to the status quo is to gain access to the system, it will probably have to come in by a side door, possibly as an instructional program for students either so far advanced or so far behind their peers that their test scores are of little concern.

That possible path to acceptance lay behind the creation of *Connections: Investigating Reality,* the model-based, online course of study accompanying this book.

There are, of course, teachers in every discipline who understand the problems and limitations of the core curriculum. For them, a few comments about possible uses of the Model may be helpful.

HISTORY

Perhaps in part because historians have often promised more from the study of history than its study usually delivers, the perceived importance of the subject has declined over the last several decades. It's still, however, a mainstay of the curriculum. Students are exposed to it at every level, and great faith is placed in its ability to do something educationally worthwhile. Advertising brochures for history textbooks say their use will "provide a sense of the past," or "give insight into the roots of the contemporary situation." "Making the past come alive" is also often cited as an outcome of study.

There's value in these kinds of objectives of historical study, but whether what actually happens in history classrooms does indeed make the past come alive, provides a sense of it, or gives insight into the roots of the contemporary situation, is highly questionable. There's considerable evidence that in fact nothing much at all of lasting consequence results from most students' several years' exposure to historical information. Some maintain that the benefits of such study are too subtle to evaluate, but the argument is weak. If the supposed benefits come from a knowledge of past events, and few of those events can be recalled by most people once the threat of the final exam no longer looms, it's hard to support the claim. Add to that the fact that, for good reason, students regularly rate history as one of the most boring subjects they've been required to take. That's further evidence that, for most learners, little of lasting benefit comes from its study.

Refresh your memory with a few textbook-style sentences found in Figure 3.1.

There's a story there, but it really *is* boring. What makes a story a *good* one—the idiosyncrasies of the teller, the subjectivity, the undisguised speculation, the intentional exaggeration, the emotional peaks, the humor—are missing, because including them would have gotten the book thrown out by the textbook selection committee. Consistent with Schoolmaster Gradgrind's philosophy, history textbook selection committees are looking for *facts*. Lots of them. Textbooks, like encyclopedias, aren't supposed to have "style." But take the personality of the writer out of a story and what's left, as some historian once said, is mostly "one damned thing after another."

The Americans signed, in 1783, a treaty with England recognizing the independence of the United States. England agreed with this generous treaty because, being at war with three countries at the moment, it decided to end the American drain on its military strength.

A war cannot, by itself, solve all the issues that bring it on.

Figure 3.1.

That's too bad, because a good tale, well told, has much in common with a musical composition. Its value lies beyond rational explanation. It's good because it's interesting or beautiful or inspirational, good not because of what it helps us know but in how it makes us feel. Reading or listening to a good story is an esthetic experience. There's no more reason to weigh the experience down with a requirement that the details be memorized to prepare for a test than there is to require those who attend symphony orchestra concerts to hum compositions before granting that their listening experience was successful.

To merely make the past come alive, to acquire some sense of it, or to seek in it only the roots of the contemporary situation, is to make minimal use of its potential. As film makers and a few teachers with the rare knack of story telling demonstrate, it can be a source of great entertainment. But to chase only the narrow objectives possible when it's organized in story form is an enormous waste.

That said, if "remembering the story" is considered important, the Model introduced in Part Two is invaluable. American history as it's usually taught inundates learners with information far beyond their ability to cope. The Model provides major organizing ideas that display the "big picture" and make clear major patterns and regularities in human affairs that aid both understanding and memory.

The Model also deals in depth with system change. Rather obviously, investigating the dynamics of the change process requires looking into the past. Thus, *a study of history is an absolute necessity if we're to make sense of the world in which we live.*

But using the past as a learning resource requires something other than the standard history textbook. These ordinarily offer learners pre-digested, often over-simplified analyses of the past, short-circuiting learner opportunities for challenging thought.

If, however, learners are given primary sources—the real-world "residue" of a past reality—making sense of them requires learners to bring to bear every known thought process, plus, perhaps, a bit of emotion. When the author of a 600 or 700-page history textbook includes a sentence saying life on the American frontier was hard, it's likely that nothing at all of consequence happens in the mind of the learner. But if that author allows George Washington to say something on the matter in his own words, written in his diary as he surveyed northern Virginia beyond the Blue Ridge Mountains, that's far less likely to be the case.

> Tuesday, March 15th, 1747. We set out early with Intent to Run round ye sd land but being taken in a Rain & Increasing very fast obliged us to return, clearing about one o'clock & our time being too Precious to Loose we a second time ventured out & Worked hard till Night & then return'd to Pen-

ningtons we got our Suppers & was Lighted into a room & I not being so good a Woodsman as ye rest of my Company striped myself very orderly & went in to ye Bed as they called it when to my Surprise I found it to be nothing but a Little Straw—-matted together without Sheets or anything else but only one thread Bear blanket with double its weight of Vermin such as Lice Fleas &c I was glad to get up (as soon as y Light was carried from us) I put on my Cloths and Lays as my Companions. Had we not have been very tired I am sure we would not have slep'd much that night I made a Promise not to Sleep so from that time forward chusing rather to sleep in y. open air before a fire as will appear hereafter.

(Further comments about the merit of first-hand or primary sources follow in Part Four.)

The past can be a major source of understanding of ourselves, the society of which we're a part, and the attitudes of others toward us. It can expand our freedoms and stimulate our creativity. It can, in fact, contribute in very specific and very powerful ways to the achievement of every major objective of general education. But it can't do that if a chronological narrative is the only form in which it's handed to learners.

The Model opens the door to many different approaches to studying the past. Most narrative-style histories devote the most pages to politics and economics—patterns for exercising power and distributing wealth. The Model points to many other patterns that make up a people's way of life.

All societies' stories follow a plot laid down by their shared ideas as they act, interact, and relate to their sub-societies and other societies. However, most textbooks simply describe the action, either ignoring the ideas and assumptions driving it or assuming those states of mind are just human nature. The Model asks, "What were these people *thinking* that caused them to do what they did?"

Historians often refer to "the dynamics of historical change," but let it go at that, offering no comprehensive, systematic explanation of how or why things change. The Model provides a framework applicable to any society in any era.

Cut through all the clutter of words of historical accounts, and the search for an answer to two simple, direct questions can keep study on track: "Who are these people we're trying to understand?" and, "How did they become who they are?" The questions may seem vague and general, but using the Model as a template, they can be answered with a precision and comprehensiveness far beyond what's otherwise possible.

In the study of American history, some may think the "who are these people?" question can be ignored. Americans are, well, Americans. But not until students have some understanding of Americans' shared ideas— their unexamined assumptions and beliefs about themselves, each other, time, nature, causation, the good life, and other important, shared states of mind—and have given thought to how those states of mind shaped what happened, has history instruction met its responsibility.

THE SOCIAL SCIENCES

The social sciences play a fairly minor role in the traditional curriculum. History, as it's usually taught, belongs in the humanities department, and economics, cultural geography, political science, sociology, anthropology, and so on, if offered, are almost always electives.

Considering that most of the really difficult individual and collective problems faced by humankind stem in one way or another from human interaction, this doesn't seem to make good sense. In mathematics, language, natural science, and other fields, students move year by year through more or less integrated, articulated, increasingly complex conceptual sequences. But in the study of *ourselves,* in the one area where ignorance and misunderstanding are the most costly and dangerous, it seems to be assumed that common sense and a little history provide students with all the understanding they need. Little or no attempt is ordinarily made to coordinate or integrate social science courses either with each other or with other parts of the curriculum.

The Model solves that problem easily and efficiently. We organize ourselves into groups—families, teams, congregations, schools, legislatures, corporations, societies, nations, civilizations. These are systems, and the social sciences are studies of various subsystems of those systems—subsystems for distributing wealth, making decisions, controlling deviance, producing goods. Social studies at the elementary level, history, economics, civics, world geography, government, and sociology at the secondary level, and all the social sciences at the college level could (and should) become parts of a single, integrated discipline. It's easy to be overwhelmed by the bulk and apparent randomness of the social sciences, but if they're recognized as attempts to make more sense of subsystems of whole social systems, and those wholes are kept constantly in view, not only do the subsystems make more sense, they also become mutually supportive.

What contribution can the Model make to the study of, say, economics? It helps learners understand what many professional economists don't yet adequately appreciate, that economics can only be understood in the context of the total system. Economic behavior is behavior inextricably linked to *all* the attributes of a particular society—environment, actors, action, and shared ideas—and their interrelationships.

What, for example, could be more central to accurate economic prediction than knowing that the number of actors in a particular age group is declining, that a weather cycle is likely to mean years of decreased rainfall in an area, that the number of single-parent households is growing, or that ideas about what constitutes the good life are increasingly concerned with self-sufficiency?

That's the kind of information to which the Model draws direct attention. Expanding awareness of such factors won't make the student an economist (that's not the goal), but it puts the subject in perspective, shows very clearly how it relates to other school subjects, identifies major variables in economic behavior, demonstrates that expansion of economic thought occurs through the exploration of relationships, and identifies relevant factors involved in economic prediction. That's a reasonably good foundation for later specialization if a learner is so inclined.

The same thing is true for every field of study. Buckminster Fuller told an audience meeting in Rockford, Illinois in the late 1980s that American education had evolved in such a way it would "be the undoing of the society." He was referring to the fact that higher education channels the best minds into ultra-specializations, one consequence of which is that political, economic, and social institutions are often led by second-rate leaders who can't see "the big picture," don't understand that highly specialized education might actually be *causing* problems. Millions of experts doing their thing with little or no understanding of how their actions interact invites new and serious problems.

Custom and bureaucracy limit possibilities, but even in general social science courses the Model can display the systemic forest, of which a particular course is a tree. Whether the whole of which that tree is part is large, small, simple, complex, transitory, long-lived, contemporary, ancient, or primitive, makes no particular difference. The aim is to send the learner off better able to make sense of experience, better able to identify that which is relevant, understanding not just the content of the traditional social sciences but much else that's essential to sense making. The Model provides a conceptual structure for scientific study that's intellectually manageable by average learners of at least the upper-elementary level, yet is complex enough to challenge the adult mind. It's dynamic, for it generates the hypotheses that lead to its own elaboration and expansion; it provides a conceptual base appropriate for the specializations of existing and yet-to- be-developed social sciences; it establishes concrete criteria for content selection; and it equips the student with a conceptual structure that integrates the social sciences with the rest of the general studies curriculum.

THE HUMANITIES

Academic disciplines are supported by arguments that try to explain or justify their inclusion in the curriculum, usually in the form of statements of goals or educational objectives. Of all the traditional areas of study, none has statements of instructional objectives more abstract and lofty than those coming from humanities literature. Humanities courses, the textbook preface may say, will "increase human potential," provide a "basis for formulating a philosophy of life," "enhance self-awareness," be "a source of insight into humanness," or "contribute to the development of perceptual and imaginative skills needed to understand experience."

Those are admirable objectives, but move from the prefaces to the bodies of most humanities textbooks, and the earlier claims tend to slip out of sight. If routine course content relates at all, it does so in such subtle ways that the two probably won't actually meet in most students' minds. The best-selling textbooks in the field concern themselves primarily with "styles," "movements," "schools," and "periods" of artistic production. Text and graphics describe and interpret works that, using various criteria, are perceived as belonging together. How those get translated into earlier promises of intellectual or emotional benefits almost certainly isn't clear to most learners.

Humanities instruction is what it actually is in working classrooms, but it could be more—an experience far more closely aligned to the soaring language in the introductions to humanities textbooks. In the pursuit of abstract objectives, the Model provides specific, concrete direction. Humanities objectives generally reflect the view that humanness is acquired and individuals grow into it gradually as experience is evaluated and responses to certain questions are fashioned—questions such as, "Who am I? What would it be like to be someone else? What does it mean to be human? How can I make more sense of the world? How can I be more free? What are my responsibilities? How am I related to others? To nature? To time? Why do I perceive this as ugly and that as beautiful?"

The Model, particularly that part having to do with shared ideas, gives learners very direct help with these questions. It tells them they're products of a particular culture or society, a system that predisposes them to act and think in certain ways and feel those ways of acting and thinking are generally superior, or at least preferable, to other ways of thinking and acting. It tells them that the social system of which they're a part has invented certain answers to questions about the nature of the self, of existence and freedom, and about one's "proper" relationship to nature, time, and space. It tells them they'll tend to accept without question most of the beliefs, values, and assumptions of their native society, because those ideas are so deeply embedded in their minds and so reinforced by their language and ways of acting they have difficulty even imagining alterna-tives. In short, the first contribution of the Model to the attainment of abstract humanities instructional objectives is that it helps learners see how personal experience, focused by and filtered through the peculiar lens of the society within which they've grown up, has shaped them.

Formal use of the Model can lead directly to the achievement of the high-est level of humanities objectives. Ordinarily, however, these objectives are assumed to be pursued indirectly, as learners engage in the day-to-day task of trying to understand, organize, and interpret the art, architecture, music, literature, and other creative effort of different peoples and eras.

For this task, the Model provides a comprehensive conceptual frame-work or template. It establishes the elementary and important fact that creativity can only be understood from "inside," in terms established by the society or social system of which the creator is or was a member. What's written or painted or designed means only what those within a particular system intend it to mean. A dance isn't just a dance, it's what-ever those who devise it, perform it, or watch make of it. The very same movement may, in the context of one society, be an act of worship, in another have sexual meaning, in yet another may be designed to manipu-late the spirit world. There's no way to know what's meant simply by look-ing at the thing created, nor is there any way for outsiders to see it in just the way it's seen by those within the originating society. The most the out-sider can do is speculate about its meaning, and the only valid approach to that is to try to grasp the totality of the social system of which the cre-ation is or was a part.

The Model also helps learners understand that dance, music, litera-ture, sculpture, painting, architecture, language, village design, philo-sophical system, and everything else within a particular society will tend to be more or less consistent or integrated. All will be products of the basic shared ideas and values of that system. The East Indian musical composition, for example, moving along without pause, without climax, with little change in tempo or dynamics, is perfectly in tune with funda-mental premises of traditional Indian society.

The Model helps guide study of members of other societies, individu-als very likely to have different assumptions about life, self, time, causa-tion, and so forth. It points out that many ways of acting and thinking aren't just different but may also be interesting, beautiful, complex, logi-cal, valid, and useful. As this happens, awareness of differences clarifies thinking about one's own ways of acting and thinking and opens up myr-iad possibilities for alternatives. One can begin to appreciate the exciting and challenging fact that there are endless ways of being human, and that some of the alternatives may be more realistic or more satisfying than those one calls one's own. When that happens, freedom expands, other humanities objectives begin to be realized, self-awareness is heightened, and perception of the range of human potential is broadened.

For the teacher designing or revising a humanities course, all previous discussion concerning the role of the Model is applicable. It's a device that's about as simple as the task permits for helping students see the wholes of which individual creations are projections or manifestations. Its use will, of course, require class time that might otherwise be used to "cover the material," but the benefits surely far exceed the costs.

For the teacher willing to think freshly about the content and organization of humanities instruction, The Model will suggest other possibilities—alternatives to present practice that both allow the highest-order, most general humanities objectives to be pursued in systematic, concrete fashion, and place the traditional content in contexts making it more manageable, memorable, and useful.

LANGUAGE

Every academic discipline can be strengthened by clarifying its cultural base and fitting its conceptual structure within the largest possible knowledge framework. In the study of language, however, this process is hardly necessary. The structure of a language and the culture of its native speakers are so tightly interwoven they can't be separated. Each "creates" the other. Every insight into a language opens a window on the society of which it's a part, and every insight into that society opens a window on its language. We may not choose to look through the windows, or we may not yet be perceptive enough to interpret what we see, but the windows are there.

The potential contribution of the Model to increased understanding of language is great. Unfortunately, that potential will often be ignored because day-to-day decisions about language instruction may take precedence. Teachers, of course, want their charges to learn to speak, read, and write their own or another language correctly, and to that end, spelling is tested, vocabulary exercises are assigned, reading is practiced, speeches are made, essays are written, and grammar is studied. In each activity the teacher's role is often much the same—to point out deviations from whatever is thought to be correct. Larger matters are often neglected: coming to see language as an interesting phenomenon, a complex puzzle, a source of insight into self, a key to how the mind works, a map to guide the study of familiar and unfamiliar societies. When that's the case, the Model will seem unrelated to language study. If the aim is for language learners to merely "rehearse" the language until they get it right, there's no need for conceptual tools designed to increase understanding.

Of these two emphases—learning a language and understanding language—the latter ought surely to occupy a place equal to the former in the general education curriculum. What could be more central to general education than a study of language, since without it, humanness is impossible? That we make so little effort to deepen our understanding of what sets us so far apart from most other creatures is a question that students in language classes ought to be led to think about.

There are others: What's a "word"? How many kinds are there? What's a "sentence"? What does it mean to "know" a language? What does "correct language" mean? Who decides? On what basis?

Every language exists in many styles and sub-styles—a style for speaking with close friends, for example, and within this style, variations that depend on age, gender, and situation. There are styles related to status, public address, speaking to one's self, public speaking on solemn occasions, styles for talking to gods or spirits, telling secrets, and many, many others. How many such styles can be identified? How do they differ? Why? Under what circumstances is each used? What are the consequences in different situations of using a wrong style?

Within the same language, subtle variations in speech can mean the difference between acceptance and rejection, success and failure. What are those variations? Where are they found? What purposes do they serve? Why are such differences often deliberately maintained or even emphasized in the face of apparently negative consequences?

Does a language bias its users' perceptions of experience, encouraging, facilitating, or even requiring certain ways of thinking and discouraging, making difficult or impossible other ways of thinking? Are some languages better than others? More suitable for some purposes or in some situations than other languages? Which purposes or situations?

Why do languages change? Are there patterns in or directions to the changes? Does language make social change more or less difficult? Why? Are changes in language resisted? If so, by whom? When? How? Why? Why do those who speak two languages sometimes have feelings of language inadequacy, while those who speak only one language don't?

The move from language "mechanic" to "language scientist," from language "insider" to "outsider," from language as something to learn to language as something to raise difficult questions about, may seem to some a poor use of time, but only if making more sense of experience isn't considered the overarching aim of a general education.

Students have to function in a world in which their skill in the use of language has real and important consequences, so language understanding shouldn't be at the expense of language facility, but mere facility sells the subject short. Language study needs to be put in perspective, and the Model can help.

THE NATURAL SCIENCES

Black holes in space. Music. The nature of smell. Bacteria that thrive on the sea floor at temperatures and pressures greater than those in a laboratory autoclave. The incredibly complex collective behavior of certain insects ...

To mysteries such as these there's literally no end. Any randomly chosen bit of the universe encloses puzzles beyond count, and the pursuit of understanding increases rather than diminishes their number. Around such mysteries a never-ending curiosity-driven course of study can be assembled, a study that begins in infancy and, unless killed by deadly instruction, extends for a lifetime.

That kind of study belongs in the schools. Science is often sold as necessary to meet the needs of American industry or keep the nation ahead of the international competition, but the best reason to study mysteries is because they exist. We're born curious, and probing what we don't know is human and fulfilling. It's also the foundation of basic research, the unexpected results of which often prove beneficial in unexpected ways. School science shouldn't have boundaries. Anything and everything is potentially exciting and important.

But there are certain aspects of the natural world that it's imperative to understand not simply because they're challenging or fun, but also because the nature and quality of our lives, and sometimes life itself, depend on understanding. The average person can probably afford a degree of ignorance about, say, optical phenomena or the composition of the rings of Saturn, but should know as much as possible about aspects of the physical world that are linked to personal or social well-being or that affect or have the potential to affect ways of life.

The focus of that "personally relevant" science is sharp, but its scope isn't narrow. Anything that alters or is likely to alter the characteristics of a society's actors or environment, thereby exerting pressure on its important ways of acting or its shared ideas, needs to be identified and monitored, and its implications understood. Biological, technological, physiological, and environmental changes need to be continuously observed and analyzed. A region's water table dropping a centimeter a year or taking ever longer to recover, a growing season decreasing by a few days each century, a gradual change in the composition of the atmosphere, the steady depletion of a nonrenewable resource, the gradual appearance or disappearance of a particular organism in the ocean—these are the kinds of changes which, unnoticed, can cause human societies to shudder, bend, or disintegrate, with those whose lives are changed or ended perhaps never knowing the sources of their trauma.

A science that grows out of an attempt to identify and monitor these kinds of changes and determine their actual and potential impact on social systems should be part of an integrated general education curriculum. A systems-based approach, using analytical categories such as those stated early in Part Two, is essential.

MATHEMATICS

Making change, computing gas mileage, balancing a checkbook, figuring how much kitchen tile is needed—all kinds of daily, mundane activities require the use of mathematics. It's an indispensable tool, one that schools must help every learner acquire.

The value and frequency of use of simple mathematical concepts and skills, however, can lead to some questionable assumptions about the place of mathematics in the curriculum. Because some mathematics is obviously a good thing, it doesn't necessarily follow that, for purposes of general education, more is better. Certainly students with mathematical ability should be helped to move as far as they can go as fast as they can go, but that's no less than should be done for those who can sing, dance, write computer programs, build beautiful tables, or generate promising hypotheses about the cause of a disease. The general education component of the curriculum shouldn't be shaped, as it now is, by considerations of the academic potential of one segment of the student population, or by pressures from business and industry or others to cut general education short by premature efforts to specialize.

In defense of extensive mathematical study, one old argument is that it contributes to "mental discipline" or that it develops "logical processes." Research hasn't borne out either contention, but even if it had, the mechanical nature of much instruction makes such benefits unlikely to be realized in the average classroom.

Mathematics instruction—a great deal of it—should be available. But for general education, once students have acquired the simple concepts and skills daily functioning requires, the mathematics needed is the mathematics that helps make sense of experience. What important characteristics of a system's population can be quantified, what are the numbers, and how are they changing? What's happening to a system's environment, to its wealth, climate, resources, and tools? Which ways of acting are followed by how many, and how are action patterns changing? Which actors believe what? How strongly?

Answers to questions like these help to put our situations in perspective and increase our control over our fates. Mathematics needs to be taken out into the real world—not simply out to concerns about balancing checkbooks and making change, but to all dimensions of reality. There's much in daily experience that, in the absence of concepts for dealing with its quantitative aspects, eludes understanding. To see clearly the shape of the present, the curves of history, the probable and possible contours of the future, mathematical ideas are essential. What students need isn't game playing with numbers, but conceptual tools for making more sense of what's happening, and why. Mathematics needs to expand understanding of the real world, needs to get off the pages of textbooks and be put to work taking our measure and the measure of the world around us, helping us understand what's happening, when, where, and with what intensity and frequency. To that end mathematics is indispensable. To simply play with it, or hand it to students because some people find the puzzles it presents interesting or challenging, is irresponsible.

It's also irresponsible to make courses in "higher math" mandatory. No one benefits thereby. The very small percentage of students who show real promise in mathematics are done a disservice when they're put in classes with promising surgeons, diesel mechanics, social workers, and so on, and so are those promising surgeons, mechanics, and social workers. Some vague notion of "rigor" that fills specialized classes with those for whom the work is irrelevant has done great harm to students, teachers, taxpayers, and the larger society. It's also a factor contributing to dropout rates and the population of the nation's prisons.

SPECIAL CLASSES

Non-Native Students

Modern travel, changes in the distribution of wealth, political turmoil, and other factors have resulted in considerable increases in the number of students from other cultures enrolled in American schools and universities. The problems are about what one would expect—difficulties with the language, teacher use of explanatory allusions not understood by those reared elsewhere, content inappropriate for or inapplicable to life in other societies, ethnocentric biases in instruction and instructional materials, instructional objectives and evaluations put in place without consideration for nontraditional students. Problems are sometimes less marked in technical fields, but not in general education. This is where the most difficulties arise, the most student potential is wasted, and the richest opportunities for both foreign and native students are left unexplored and unexploited.

Given a reasonable degree of teacher flexibility, the Model can help with all these problems. Used as a basis for a special class or incorporated into traditional general education courses, it becomes a means to the achievement of the full range of objectives already identified. It can tailor the general education program to the individual student and make that program as valid and useful for the foreign student who returns home as it is for American students. It can help non-natives make more sense of America and its various subcultures, and make the foreign student a real classroom asset, for the Model is a vehicle for comparative societal study. Both foreign and native students can serve as sources of systematically organized information in classroom explorations of each other's societies, explorations that enlighten and broaden both those who ask and those who answer questions. It provides unparalleled opportunities for first-hand experience. What's necessary to take advantage of the opportunities this contact presents for intellectual and emotional growth is a reasonably culturally neutral guide to channel communication and structure understanding. The Model serves that purpose.

Foreign Travel

Students who travel abroad to observe unfamiliar contemporary societies or to see the preserved artifacts of earlier societies face the same conceptual problems as students of history, new employees in a corporation, archeologists, cultural anthropologists, and new residents in town. They're flooded with tremendous amounts of raw data to sort out, assign meaning and priority, relate, and integrate to form an understandable picture of an unfamiliar social system. The similarity of this task to those previously discussed should make apparent the applicability and usefulness of the Model in travel abroad. Like the childhood puzzle in which a picture begins to emerge as numbered dots are connected with lines, the outlines of unfamiliar societies begin to emerge as the information called for by the Model is identified. It doesn't provide a map of the unfamiliar, but it does provide guidelines for making one. It also reminds the student that much that's novel or exotic may be of little or no significance in the attempt to make sense of an unfamiliar society.

Institutional Orientation

It was suggested earlier that a major weakness in the traditional curriculum is its failure to help learners understand those institutions that structure their daily lives, institutions having much to do with their well-being, happiness, and success. We don't ordinarily "step outside" our religious, economic, political, social, and educational organizations and observe with the critical and objective eye that distance provides. We tend, for example, to see schools and universities merely as sources of what might be called "standard services," rather like educational vending machines. How they work is of little interest or consequence as long as they continue to provide the expected services. We're vaguely aware that someone loads the machine, that some kind of mechanism responds to the coins or the kick and thereupon delivers the goods, but preoccupied by the fare being delivered, the machine itself is taken for granted and largely ignored.

This ought not to be. The appropriateness of the choices our schools provide, how those choices are made, how much they cost and why, are part of the transaction. They need to be understood. And the customer, the school, and those in charge of it, will be better off if they *are* understood by the learners they're supposed to serve.

In vending machines, wear and obsolescence are natural and inevitable. They're constantly being rebuilt and redesigned. In education, as was pointed out in the Introduction, increasing program inefficiency and obsolescence are equally natural and inevitable. And, just as it's desirable that in the redesign of vending machines the customers, engineers, designers, service personnel, repairers, and others contribute to its improvement, so it is that schools, legislatures, courts, religious groups, and other institutions can be improved by the suggestions of all those who affect and are affected by them.

Before that can happen, however, the workings of the machine as it is must be exposed. Inspection plates, covers, and housings must be removed (usually over the protests of those who've come to feel that the machines are their exclusive property and that therefore their nature and functioning are no one else's business). When the workings are open to view and study, then some kind of guide or handbook is needed. In an orientation to the educational "machines" we've created, the Model can serve that purpose. Although other conceptual schemes for analyzing the structure and functioning of schools are available, two arguments favor its use.

First, if the Model is already being used to organize a general education course, applying it to a different, constantly accessible chunk of the real world reinforces and strengthens the concepts it teaches. Humanities, language, history, the social sciences, and detailed study of the school itself become mutually supportive. Second, the Model is a better guide than the catalogs, public relations brochures, media releases, organizational charts, and the explanations of those in charge in making sense of how the institution is structured and how it functions. Some discomfort may result if students begin to ask questions about environments, about, say, the design of a new wing, the shared ideas of those who made the decisions, the actions that translated their decisions into a final form, and so on, but the interests of students, the institution, and the larger society will in the long run be served. Discussion of the implications of the relative size and decor of the offices of various institutional employees, of budget items and the priorities they reflect, of ways for displaying status or authority—indeed of all aspects of the school as they're surfaced by the Model—can, if properly focused, provide learners with concrete illustrations of every one of its elements. Students can learn first-hand how one complex system *really* works, and in turn help that institution and others to which they belong meet their most important objectives—sustained effectiveness through self-renewal.

LIMITATIONS OF THE MODEL

The constant repetition of the phrase "the Model can ..." has almost certainly become tiresome. It should be clear, however, that *it's not the attributes of the Model, but the ubiquitousness of what it models* that makes it so broadly applicable. Other models of organized human groups can also demonstrate the unfortunate arbitrariness and awkwardness of the boundaries we've created between fields of knowledge, but the naturalness and simplicity of the one all humans routinely use are surely assets. Many years of experimentation have proved it to be a practical, workable tool. Thousands of students of differing age, ability, nationality, cultural heritage, and academic levels have used it to study neighborhoods, corporations, nations, ethnic groups, ancient civilizations, utopian and fictional societies, religious movements, city-states, tribes, ships' crews, schools, military installations, athletic teams, youth gangs, revolutionaries, and other human groups. It's been used to structure comparative studies of rural and urban subcultures, to trace differences between "town and gown," to contrast those living on "opposite sides of the railroad track," to clarify conflicts and misunderstanding between various groups, and as a basis for counseling marriage partners of differing cultural background. That its use hasn't spread is due primarily to institutional inertia, bureaucratic rigidities, simplistic standards and accountability measures, distrust of the judgment of educators, and narrow policies put in place by those in authority who know little about educating.

As with all models, however, this one creates for its users a potentially serious problem. Although new models of the real world liberate and expand thinking, they also eventually begin to have negative effects. What begins as *a* way of modeling reality in order to make it intellectually manageable tends increasingly to become *the* way of doing so. Instead of checking our models against reality to see how they should be changed to make them more accurate and useful, we tend to accept only information that fits with or reinforces the one we've come to find comfortable and useful. The longer we use a particular model, the harder it becomes to change or discard it.

We can try to build in obstacles to this tendency. To begin with, the fact that the use of the Model is conscious and deliberate remind us that it's merely a model and shouldn't be allowed to structure thinking too rigidly. Second, its categories are very general and allow considerable latitude for interpretation and application. Finally, if ever the importance of the holistic study of systems in particular and societies in general is appreciated, it's likely that alternative models and variations on those models will be constantly appearing. The more there are, the less likely is it that any one of them will become rigidly institutionalized. The teacher can also contribute to flexibility by making it clear that a model is merely a starting point, a temporary structure to be constantly torn apart and rebuilt as experience and analysis suggest ever more useful forms. Model evolution can also be encouraged by presenting aspects of reality that don't fit comfortably into the model being used and challenging students to reconcile the two.

Incidentally, activities such as this can serve another valuable purpose, demonstrating that human systems are inherently the most complex and challenging entities known, and worthy of the best efforts of the best students. It's ironic that social studies, the elementary- and secondary-level school subject that by title would seem to come nearest to being a study of the complexity of humankind and the human condition, is regularly ranked by students as the least challenging area of study. As a consequence, many who might eventually be able to contribute much to our understanding of ourselves and others turn for intellectual stimulation to fields thought, incorrectly, to be more intellectually challenging.

PART FOUR

NOTES ON TEACHING

I began playing with models for human systems in the 1960s, while teaching interdisciplinary social science at Florida State University. Since then, I've worked with students at every level from elementary school through the university, students representing the range of abilities, interests, and inclinations found in most public schools and colleges. I've taught in a half-dozen different institutions in several different fields. I've administered, observed, consulted, supervised, and coordinated. I've written articles, textbooks, professional books, and instructional programs. For seven years, I wrote nationally distributed newspaper columns on education for Knight-Ridder/Tribune Information Services.

Nevertheless, I'm reluctant to give advice, except in a very general way. Here's the text of my Knight-Ridder/Tribune column for the *Orlando Sentinel* newspaper for the 21st of September, 2002:

> Maybe she's still playing the piano and enjoying it. Maybe not. But if she is, she and her mother probably have my oldest son to thank.
>
> He was back from the U.S. Navy. He'd served his hitch as a musician, sometimes playing trombone in big bands, but more often playing upright bass or guitar in small combos, backing up touring entertainers.
>
> He hadn't yet gone into the civil-engineering field, and was picking up miscellaneous work ranging from carpentry to filling in at a

What's Worth Learning?
pp. 89–107
Copyright © 2011 by Information Age Publishing

local music store. He preferred the part-time store job, especially giving music lessons. The pay was poor, but the satisfactions great.

The little girl came in trailing her mother by several steps. She had a book of beginner-level keyboard exercises under her arm and a scowl on her face.

The mother explained that, although she herself wasn't an accomplished pianist, playing had always given her pleasure and she wanted that for her daughter. She had, however, about given up. Would someone at the store at least give it a try?

"Sure," said my son. He made some get-acquainted small talk with the 7-year-old, then took her hand and led her to a practice room.

"Do you like that book under your arm?" "No," she answered.

"I didn't think so. Want to pitch it?" my son asked.

"Yes," she said, brightening considerably.

"OK. Put it over there, come sit beside me, and let's try something. I'm going to play a chord—hit a bunch of notes all at once. When I do, you fool around with one finger until you find a note that sounds good to you when you hear it with the notes I'm playing."

There was initial uncertainty, but she found a groove. After several minutes of this he said, "OK. Here's what I want you to do this week. First, put your book in the bench at home and forget about it. Then, I want you to try to make up a little tune. Like this. Or this. Or this." With one finger, he played three short, funky, unfamiliar little melodies.

"When you have one you like, bring it back ready to play for me next week. Oh, and give your tune a name," he added. "OK?"

He told the mother not to let her spend more than 15 minutes a day at the piano. The mother said she couldn't imagine that keeping her daughter away from the keyboard would be difficult.

I'm sure I've remembered all this because, although my son had few formal music lessons himself, I've long considered his approach to be a useful model of sound education.

First, he did an aptitude check. Watching and listening as the little girl found notes that fit the chords he played, he settled to his own satisfaction that she didn't have a tin ear. If he'd thought that, he'd have gently suggested to the mother that maybe her daughter's talents lay elsewhere, maybe in dance or art or some other field.

That's not how it is in America's schools. Aptitude or lack of it is irrelevant. There's a required curriculum. If you want to graduate, you have to pass, for example, algebra. Period.

Second, he individualized the instructional material. The little girl's tune, not those in her book, was the focus of instruction.

That's not how it is in America's schools. Textbooks are the primary focus of instruction—pre-processed content assembled by publishers with an eye on what they think will sell in their two biggest markets, Texas and California.

Third, he moved her gradually through increasing levels of complexity. When she came back the next week, he wrote out her tune on large manuscript paper, with the title she'd chosen at the top. As the weeks passed, her little tune was elaborated. The single line of melody became a progression of chords—a composition.

Fourth, there were no grades, no gold stars. He relied on intrinsic rather than extrinsic motivation. This was her tune and her increasing elaboration of it, with all the satisfaction accompanying creativity and ownership. She wasn't just taking piano lessons, she was writing music. She was a composer!

Ironic. When it comes to cranking out slogans and bumper stickers about individualism and "doing it my way," America surely ranks near the top in volume of production. In our schools, however, we demand "accountability" for turning out super-standardized kids.

Go figure.

*   *   *

Individual differences in students, differences in ethnic and regional backgrounds, differences in teacher personality and philosophy, in level of maturity of an academic discipline, in instructional materials, in administrative style and presence, in physical facilities, and much else, convince me that I'm unlikely to be able to give usefully precise advice about how to teach. I'm most comfortable, therefore, in saying, "Here are some thoughts I've had and some approaches I've tried in my efforts to expand student understanding of their experience." Maybe my comments will give readers some useful ideas. They might also make policymakers more aware of the utter futility of trying to control what happens in classrooms by means of top-down mandates. Rarely do those do more than expose the naïveté of those who framed them. Altering what happens in others' minds is far too complex a process to be effectively directed by state legislatures or Congress.

Preliminaries

I walk into my classes on the first day aware that my approach to teaching is idiosyncratic (as it is with all teachers). Since students may find my classes different, and since humans sometimes react negatively to the unfamiliar, I try to identify the peculiarities of my teaching style and make both my idiosyncrasies and the students' possible reactions to them matters of thorough discussion. The relationship of student to teacher isn't ordinarily a casual one. If it takes a few hours to establish a good working relationship, I consider the time well spent. I don't feel compelled to confront them on the first day of class with a formidable chunk of whatever we'll eventually be exploring. I'd rather visit together, finding out who they are, letting them know who I am, and discussing some of the assumptions we've brought with us, assumptions that might bear on the success (or lack of it) of our work together.

Some of these assumptions have to do with the nature of the student–teacher relationship. If I find myself in a conventional classroom with conventional furniture conventionally arranged, after we've introduced ourselves to each other and visited awhile, I may begin a discussion of our relationship by asking the students to think and talk about the implications of the place we're in. What does the furniture imply about their role? About mine? About our relationship to each other? About relative power? Where are the empty spaces, and what do they mean? Who "owns" the chalkboard and other technology, and what of that? Are the height of the ceiling, the orientation of the furniture to the entrance area, the very fact that there's such a room at all, useful to us in our attempt to understand the assumptions about education we've probably absorbed from the society of which we're a part?

And when we've noted the messages that seem to be transmitted by this environment in which we find ourselves, we question the validity of those messages. The desk, the podium, the "walking around" space for me, for example, imply authority. What sort of authority? Based on what assumptions? How valid *are* those assumptions? And so on.

Out of this comes, if at all possible, a rearranging of furniture. I'm convinced that the deepest levels of understanding come from direct, person-to-person dialog, so it follows that furniture should be arranged to make it easy for everyone to have eye contact with everyone else. I sit in that circle, and to avoid that space eventually being viewed differently than any other space, I'll take a different seat every day.

Roles

One of the messages transmitted by the arrangement of the typical classroom is that the teacher is an expert on the subject at hand, and her or his role is to distribute information. Now there are one or two matters on which I might be considered expert, but in my view the expert role is of limited value in education. I'm not interested in students leaving my class with a few hundred answers borrowed from me and soon forgotten. They don't need yesterday's or today's answers. They need tomorrow's answers, and I don't have them.

I'm much more interested in students leaving my class as *real students*—curious, probing, interested, self-propelled, alive. That seems more likely to happen if they perceive *me* as curious, probing, interested, self-propelled, and alive—being, as much as I can be, the kind of student I want them to be. Obviously this doesn't mean that I adopt student mannerisms or that I fail to meet my responsibilities in matters of bureaucratic routine. I simply want to model the kind of actions and attitudes that, if adopted, would allow my students to help themselves continue to grow for the rest of their lives.

As for my teacher role, what I need for that isn't an answer to every question. I need to have a general grasp of the major organizers and principles of the discipline, and I need to know how to ask the right questions—how to hold up a puzzling bit of reality or its residue, be certain the puzzle is understood, and wait . . .wait while the learner pokes and prods, turns the puzzle this way and that, shakes it, holds it up to the light, speculates, rejects, decides it has no solution, then suddenly sees something not seen before—a relationship, a pattern, an implication. It's sometimes harder to let students do that if the teacher is an expert on a subject.

The kinds of questions I tend to ask—questions for which I have no answers—make it easy for me to assume the role in which I'm most comfortable, that of just another inquisitive student. And they keep me from being bored.

Thinking

Most students have acquired some relatively rigid ideas about what's supposed to happen in school. Since what I do in class often doesn't jibe with their expectations, I've found it useful to warn them by sharing with them my reasons for departing from some of the traditional practices.

Sometimes I'll use a simple exercise to create a basis for discussion of one of the peculiarities of my approach to teaching. Without prior discussion, I'll ask them to write, on an unsigned scrap of paper, a couple of typical exam or quiz questions—any subject, any grade level. If they can't remember a specific question they've been asked, I'll say, "Make them up, but try to make them just the sort of questions you've grown accustomed to being asked by teachers or college professors."

I collect the responses, put them aside, and begin a discussion of what teachers mean when they say something like, "Now I don't know what you'll be doing in your *other* classes, but in *my* class, you're really going to have to *think!*

In the interests of precision in our discussion, I then help them break the word *think* down into a Benjamin Bloom-like taxonomy of specific thought processes—inferring, hypothesizing, generalizing, recalling, categorizing, synthesizing, and so on. With the taxonomy on the board, I then begin reading aloud their examples of typical examination questions, asking them to identify the specific thought process students in the class taking the quiz or exam on which the question appeared would probably have used to answer the question correctly. When they decide, I place a tally mark after the appropriate word on the board.

I've yet to be surprised by the result. About a dozen or fewer questions into the exercise, murmurs begin. It's clear that they've been led to believe that "thinking" almost always means simply "recalling." Often not a single question they submit will have required them to draw an inference, generate a hypothesis, postulate a relationship, formulate a generalization, make a value judgment, or engage in any thought process other than the recall of something read or heard in class. (I once did a content analysis of the final semester exams in all subjects in a mid-sized college with a good academic reputation, and found that approximately 88% of the questions were simple tests of short-term memory.)

I can then point out to the class that if I'm successful in engaging them in a *full* range of thought processes, they're going to be doing something they're not accustomed to doing. That leads to *another* dialog, this one about how they may react to that different, broadened task. Having learned how to play the "just remember what you've read or heard" game, it's entirely possible they may react negatively when I change the game, not necessarily making it harder, but merely different. I warn them that at least some are likely to react to the work with a vague feeling that "this isn't education."

That's a perfectly understandable reaction. After years of equating learning primarily with the simple process of storing information in memory and recalling it on demand, activities that require learners to use other thought processes may make them apprehensive and overly concerned about a final grade. Sometimes, the ones who object the most to being required to engage in a wide range of thought processes are those who've been the most successful in playing the old read-and-remember game.

Specific reactions can be anticipated. Some, after a few days, will say, "Please! Just tell us what you want us to know!" or, "We're not getting anywhere!" or, "This is so disorganized!" or, "Could we have a worksheet to fill out?" Others will react differently. Because they're not being asked to remember dozens or hundreds of bits of information, they consider the work easy or soft. Still others will feel that, for the first time, they've gotten hold of something really challenging and meaningful.

Potential problems associated with deliberate expansion and diversification of thought processes shouldn't be underestimated. Students aren't the only ones who may react negatively. Parents, other teachers, administrators, policymakers in state capitols and Washington, and many in the lucrative testing industry also often think educating is primarily a matter of moving information from those who know to those who don't—a sort of monster national game of Trivial Pursuit, the winners being those who can pencil in the most ovals on a test of what someone, somewhere happened to think was important. Some may even argue that schooling isn't *supposed* to require the young to think, that its purpose is just to provide them with "raw material" for thinking, that real thinking comes later, in college or in life.

These people aren't going to be understanding or supportive, but their fears and apprehensions are different from those of the students. They'll tend to say that what's being attempted is admirable, but the teacher's first obligation is to conform to established practice and teach to the standards. They won't use those words, of course; they will simply invoke the immediacy of the next standardized test mandated by some authority, and insist that the teacher's primary responsibility is to make certain that their students pass with the highest possible scores. The bureaucratic-corporate monster must be fed, even if the "standards" that are its fare are legitimized only by the fact that their origins are no longer identifiable.

In those situations, I try to kill two birds with one stone and use traditional course content in non-traditional ways. But if I can't, I simply identify the content most likely to be on the test and devise some way to deal with it efficiently. After we've discussed the necessity of meeting bureaucratic or societal expectations, I may direct the students to Cliff Notes or some other commercial outline, and assign that which is most likely to be on the standardized test as work for them to do on their own time. I consider our time together too valuable to waste on memory exercises.

Metaphors

Occasionally, to help prepare students for the instruction ahead, we'll talk about their conceptions of the teaching and learning process. It's very likely they share the usual metaphors about learning—that their heads are empty and knowledge is "stuff" to be somehow gotten inside them. We employ such figures of speech constantly because we know so little about how the mind really works. Eventually we stop thinking about our education-related metaphors as feeble attempts to describe something extremely complex and come to see them as accurately modeling the teaching and learning process. When that happens, activity that doesn't parallel our metaphors probably won't be seen as educational.

If our metaphors for educating were reasonably close to how learning actually occurs, there'd be few problems. Unfortunately, they're not. They imply that the process is simple, and as a consequence, central offices, state legislatures, Congress, state and federal departments, and rich, successful entrepreneurs have no qualms whatsoever about saying what they think should be "taught" to whom. Even the "how" of educating is often dictated so rigidly that authorities expect to be able to walk into a classroom knowing beforehand what page in the textbook is being studied. Some attach the euphemism "fidelity checks" to this ridiculous practice, demonstrating an appalling ignorance of just about everything having to do with teaching and learning.

That ignorance, often found in the minds of education policymakers in county offices, state capitols, and in Washington, is probably the single greatest obstacle to real progress in education.

I ask students questions about widely shared assumptions about educating: "Suppose the process isn't like sitting and being spoon fed, but more like, say, making love? Should that be the case, wouldn't actions and attitudes now considered appropriate and effective be unacceptable, maybe even have negative consequences?" The food metaphor suggests that in educating, one participant is active, the other passive. But if educating is more like making love, questions are raised about those roles. The two metaphors put in a different light questions central to educating, questions about authority, respect, passion, expertise, involvement, class size, even attendance.

Neither of the metaphors is adequate (although the second is probably more helpful than the first), so we discuss others. It may be that education, the objective of which is the expansion of understanding, is more a matter of closing a circuit, building a bridge, going inside to examine the skeleton, climbing an observation tower, forging a link, tracing a blueprint, or stacking blocks in different ways. We'll talk about a metaphor I frequently use—that of rearranging mental furniture. The word *rearranging* is helpful to me. I don't know how valid the idea is, but I seem to accomplish more if I assume that everything students need to know in order to understand the matter at hand they already know, but just don't know they know. My task is to wander around with them in their mental attics and basements, finding what's needed at the moment, bringing it out, dusting it off, examining with them how it's put together, then asking them where it could go to be in the most useful and meaningful relationship with the rest of their mental furniture.

Textbooks

To many, nothing seems more central to education than textbooks. Teachers, administrators, classrooms, laboratories, gymnasiums, chalkboards, desks, projectors, computers, notebooks—each has a place and plays a role, but for perhaps most of those involved in one way or another with educating, the textbook is considered the indispensable tool for educating.

Some measure of their perceived importance is indicated by actions and attitudes related to them. Parents demand that they be brought home from school. Many teachers won't start classes without them. Academic departments will adopt new textbooks and then spend weeks reorganizing courses, as if the change in books had somehow altered the reality the books attempt to explain. Administrators sometimes think that all books for a class should be the same, and that all classes using a book should be on approximately the same page on the same day. Elaborate and expensive procedures are devised to select textbooks, angry crowds sometimes burn them, and not infrequently the courts are asked to make judgments about them. Obviously, textbooks are considered very important.

To suggest that traditional textbooks are a major, perhaps *the* major obstacle to the achievement of educational excellence will seem to many to be nothing less than heresy. It's acceptable to find fault with them, to criticize the uninspired writing, the "dumbing down" of vocabulary, the concern for comprehensiveness at the expense of depth and clarity, their spiraling cost, their usual several years' lag behind current knowledge, the dreary sameness stemming from publisher attempts to duplicate the current best-seller, or even their ever-increasing weight. But to suggest that in most subjects, textbooks actually stand in the way of major educational improvement is to risk being labeled as too eccentric to be taken seriously.

Students have adopted society's general attitudes toward textbooks and textbook-like materials. For this reason, since I make very little use of textbooks (use them at all only under administrative duress), I have to go to considerable lengths to explain why.

One of the problems, I tell them, is the conventional textbook's expository style—the thousands of words "telling you what's true."

Typically, textbooks read like the examples in Figures 4.2 and 4.3.

What most textbooks offer is a kind of compendium of a field of study. The words in the text have been preceded by decades or centuries of thought, argument, exploration, criticism, organizing, and reorganizing.

Out of all this have come conclusions, often hundreds or thousands of them, and summaries of those conclusions provide most of the content of the usual textbook.

Now for reference purposes, such a resource can be useful, especially if there are no other accessible resources. There needs to be a handy place to store the distilled thinking of scholars within a field, and before the Internet, a book was probably the most appropriate device. The difficulties arise from the assumption that what's basically a reference work is a proper tool for instruction. It isn't. Outside the field of education, it's assumed that a serious book written to educate will dwell for its entire length on the development, illustration, and application of a single idea. Textbooks, however, present not one idea but a veritable tidal wave of them.

Writing a newspaper column on the matter, I went to my nearest middle school and borrowed their mainline-publisher eighth-grade textbooks for math, science, language arts, and American history. The "main ideas" presented, as indicated by their glossaries, totaled 1,465.

One thousand, four hundred and sixty-five! To think that in 180 instructional days, minus ten or so for testing, eighth graders could take away anything approaching an understanding of 1,465 ideas is preposterous! A few of the concepts were powerful, but nothing indicated their relative importance. Even if there had been criteria, mixing the truly powerful ideas indiscriminately with vast numbers of ideas of lesser importance, assured that none would be of lasting value. This mass of information, presented as it usually is without anything approaching an adequate knowledge-organizing conceptual framework, is simply overwhelming. The test performance of students with good short-term memories may perpetuate the notion that learning is taking place, but administering the same test a few weeks or months later would make it clear that such wasn't the case, and that a great deal of time and money had been wasted.

What students need isn't an encyclopedic overview of a field (even if they were able to cope with such a volume of information), but an understanding of how the field fits into the total scheme of things, what its main organizing ideas are, how they relate to each other, how those ideas and idea relationships are generated, evaluated, refined, and expanded, and of what use they are in making more sense of experience.

A second problem with textbooks is even more fundamental. Because the content of the conventional expository text is primarily a catalog of conclusions, all the significant thinking has already been done. It's very much like giving learners a vast crossword puzzle with all the blanks filled in. There's nothing left to do that's intellectually challenging or stimulating.

Figure 4.3 is an example of traditional textbook content, and of content in a form that requires the learner to use a wide range of thought processes of the kind underlying the expansion of knowledge. The examples are from history, but the differences they illustrate are applicable to every field of knowledge.

Textbooks that require learners to use a full range of thought processes occasionally appear. I know from first-hand experience as a writer of two that they enjoy little success. Ironically, although such textbooks allow students to learn in a manner far more natural than that permitted by conventional exposition, textbooks containing mostly primary data are considered too unorthodox to be acceptable. Until this attitude changes, until there's general understanding of the ways the usual textbooks get in the way of intellectual growth by short-circuiting most thought processes except recall, textbooks will continue to be a major obstacle to school improvement.

Textbooks can be vastly improved, but even those that move beyond the narrow bounds of traditional exposition are less-than-ideal tools for teaching. Education is, after all, about the real world. Textbooks are supposed to help explain that world—rocks, schizophrenia, inflation, language, vertebrates. In order to "two-dimensionalize" an aspect of reality sufficiently to fit it into the pages of a book, the author has to select, freeze, flatten, sterilize, organize, abstract. By the time the original is in textbook form, it's a pale, shallow shadow four or five steps removed from that which it models.

In my opinion, textbooks should be used as a primary instructional tool only when it's impossible to touch the real thing or its tangible residue. On the wall of every classroom, in letters too large to ignore, I'd like to see a quote from Alfred North Whitehead's 1916 Presidential Address to the Mathematical Association of England: "The second-handedness of the learned world is the secret of its mediocrity."

One more observation: From traditional assumptions about the usefulness of textbooks comes what must surely be the most mind-numbing of all classroom activities—"Fill in the blank." Sentences from textbooks are reproduced in workbooks or on worksheets, but with words missing. Millions of students spend dreary hours searching textbooks for parallel sentences providing the missing words. In many schools, particularly in some of the newer, sectarian ones, students may sit in individual study carrels transferring words from textbook to workbook. It's an utter waste of time and a criminal use of minds.

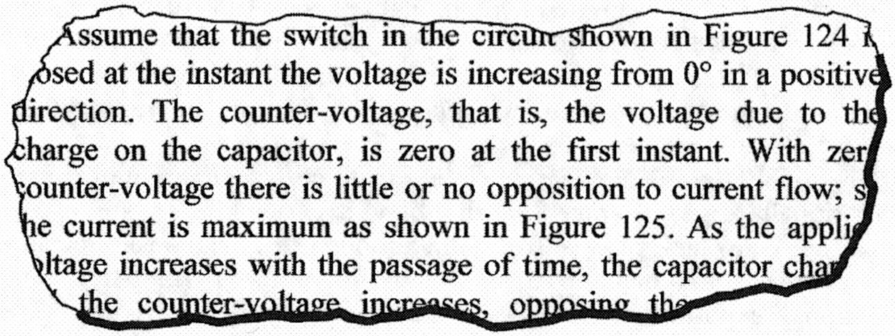

Assume that the switch in the circuit shown in Figure 124 i
osed at the instant the voltage is increasing from 0° in a positive
direction. The counter-voltage, that is, the voltage due to the
charge on the capacitor, is zero at the first instant. With zer
counter-voltage there is little or no opposition to current flow; s
he current is maximum as shown in Figure 125. As the appli
oltage increases with the passage of time, the capacitor cha
the counter-voltage increases, opposing th

Figure 4.1

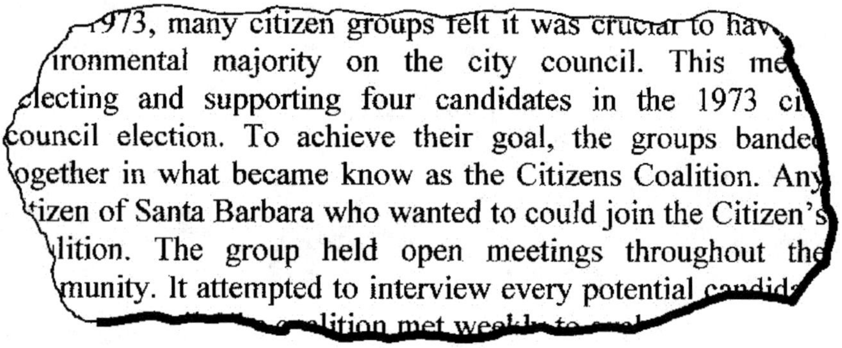

973, many citizen groups felt it was crucial to hav
ironmental majority on the city council. This me
electing and supporting four candidates in the 1973 ci
council election. To achieve their goal, the groups bande
ogether in what became know as the Citizens Coalition. An
tizen of Santa Barbara who wanted to could join the Citizen's
lition. The group held open meetings throughout the
munity. It attempted to interview every potential candid
lition met weekly to

Figure 4.2.

Conceptual Scaffolds

In earlier discussions about the inadequacies of the traditional general
education curriculum, I had much to say about its lack of conceptual
organization. We know the brain can't handle very much random information. That's why we make grocery and "to do" lists. To be stored,
recalled, and *used*, information must be placed within an organizing conceptual structure logical enough for the structure itself to lead to what's
trying to be recalled. Related ideas must be labeled and stored together in
a category, those categories labeled and stored together in more general
categories, these general categories, in turn, labeled and stored together
in still more general categories. The ultimate objective, of course, is a
totally integrated knowledge structure in which everything known is tied
together in a mutually supportive, logical framework.

Constructing such frameworks, making enough use of them to fix them in permanent place, and understanding them well enough to constantly modify them in order to align them more precisely and usefully with reality, is what educating for understanding is all about. Critics of education and most "reformers" rarely or never have anything to say about such matters, apparently assuming that if learners are simply exposed to information, in some automatic or magical way that information will self-organize and integrate. Of course, it doesn't. The theory that if you throw enough mud on the wall some of it is bound to stick is ridiculous. Instruction may dump a load of information in the student's intellectual yard, and the student may stack some of it for some particular purpose, but if a structure of consequence and permanence is built, the present curriculum deserves little credit.

Helping learners lift into consciousness and make deliberate use of their routinely used knowledge-organizing conceptual scaffold or framework is a different sort of work. In an August 24, 2010, column in the *Washington Post*, during a heated national debate about the effectiveness (or lack thereof) of the education reform proposals being promoted by mainstream media, I tried to clarify that difference:

> In alphabetical order: Mike Bloomberg, mayor of New York City. Eli Broad, financier and philanthropist. Jeb Bush, ex-Florida governor and possible 2012 presidential contender. Arne Duncan, U.S. Secretary of Education. Bill Gates, business magnate and philanthropist. Joel Klein, chancellor of New York City schools.
>
> In education issues, mainstream media sometimes call these gentlemen, "The New Progressives." They're major movers and shakers in the current reform effort.
>
> None is, or has ever been, a teacher. Many think that's a very good, even a necessary thing. It's widely believed that American education is a mess, that teachers deserve most of the blame, and that they either can't or won't clean the mess up. What's needed, it's thought, are no-nonsense leaders—CEOs from business, lawyers, politicians, ex-military officers.
>
> The New Progressives are on a roll. Their views are sought after and respected by congressional committees. They have money, and cash-starved school districts will do whatever it takes to get some of it. Their press conferences are well-attended. Most newspaper editorial boards share their perspective, so their op-eds get published. The *Common Core State Standards Initiative* they strongly supported—if not helped engineer—has already been adopted by more than half the states. Leading Democrats and Republicans are on board. Those who question their top-down approach to reform have been neutralized by labeling them "obstacles to progress," "reactionaries," "union shills."
>
> A recent press release provides an example of the New Progressives' long reach: "NBC Universal presents 'Education Nation,' an unprecedented

LEARNING ABOUT
A SOURCE OF
AMERICAN VALUES
USING EXPOSITION

What were the Puritans like? Many of their ways of acting grew out of their religious beliefs. They felt that all people were basically evil, and that only a strict observance of God's laws as presented in the Bible could keep this evil tendency under control. Attendance at Church

LEARNING ABOUT A
SOURCE OF
AMERICAN VALUES
USING "RESIDUE"

Below is the alphabet as it was taught to Puritan children in the New England Primer. What seems to be important Puritan beliefs?

In Adam's Fall
We finned all.

Thy Life to mend,
This Book attend.

The Cat doth play,
And after flay.

A Dog will bite
A Thief at Night.

An Eagle' flight
Is out of fight.

The idle Fool
Is whipt at School.

Figure 4.3.

week-long event examining and redefining education in America." The event will be held in Rockefeller Center in September, 2010. The two leaders with top billing: Bloomberg and Duncan.

The New Progressives and their fans have something else in common besides running the education reform show. They share a big idea – a theory about how humans learn.

Let's call it "Theory T." "T" stands for "Transfer."

Theory T didn't emerge from successful teaching experience, and it's not backed by research, but it has something even more useful going for it: The Conventional Wisdom. It's easily the New Progressives' most powerful asset, for much of the general public (and a disturbing percentage of teachers) already subscribe to it. Because its validity is taken for granted, Theory T doesn't even have to be explained, much less promoted.

Theory T says kids come to school with heads mostly empty. As textbooks are read, information transfers from pages to empty heads. As teachers talk, information transfers from teachers' heads to kids' heads. When homework and term papers are assigned, kids go to the library or the Internet, find information, and transfer it from reference works or Wikipedia. Bit by bit and byte, the information in their heads piles up.

At an August conference in Lake Tahoe, California, Bill Gates clinched his Theory T credentials. "Five years from now," he said, "on the web for free you'll be able to find the best lectures in the world."

Let the transfer process begin!

Measuring the success of Theory T learning is easy and precise – just a matter of waiting a few days or weeks after the transfer process has been attempted and asking the kid, "How much do you remember?"

No research says how much of what's recalled at test time remains permanently in memory, nor to what practical use, if any, that information is later put, but that's of no concern to Theory T proponents. Their interest in performance ends when the scores are posted.

There's another, less familiar theory about how humans learn. Those who subscribe to it – mostly teachers who've spent many years working directly with learners – aren't backed by big money, don't get mainstream media attention, aren't asked to testify before congressional committees, and can't organize week-long affairs in Rockefeller Plaza, all of which help explain the second theory's unfamiliarity.

Those who accept the alternative to Theory T don't think kids come to school with empty heads, believe instead that the young, on their own, develop ideas, opinions, explanations, beliefs and values about things that matter to them. As is true of adults, kids' ideas and beliefs become part of who they are, so attempts to change them may come across as attacks on their identity and be resisted.

Teaching, many long-time teachers know, isn't a simple matter of transferring information into a kid's head, but a far more complex, multi-step process. The teacher has to (a) "get inside" that head to figure out what's thought to be true, right, or important, (b) understand the kid's value system well enough to offer ideas sufficiently appealing to warrant taking them seriously and paying attention, (c) choose language or tasks that question old ideas and clarify new ones, (d) get feedback as necessary to decide how to proceed, (e) load the whole process up with enough emotion to carry it past short-term memory, and (f) do this for a roomful of kids, no two of whom are identical.

If that sounds really difficult, it's because it is. If it were easy, all kids would love school because learning is its own reward. If it were easy, young teachers would be successful and stay in the profession. If it were easy, adults wouldn't forget most of what they once supposedly learned. If it were easy, the world would be a much better place.

Most of what we know, remember, and use, we didn't learn by way of Theory T. We learned it on our own as we discovered real-world patterns and relationships – new knowledge that caused us to constantly rethink, reorganize, reconstruct, and replace earlier knowledge.

Let's call this relating process "Theory R." Theory R is why little kids learn so much so rapidly, before traditional schooling overwhelms them with Theory T. Theory R is why Socrates was famous, why project learning, internships and apprenticeships work so well, why the *real* Progressives of a hundred years ago were so adamant about "hands on" work and "learning by doing," why real dialogue in school is essential, why knowledge of a subject doesn't necessarily make a teacher effective, why asking good questions is far more important than knowing right answers, why tying national standards to a 19th Century curriculum is stupid, why standardized tests are a cruel, anti-learning, Theory T joke.

The educationally naïve New Progressives have engineered an education train wreck that, if allowed to continue, will haunt America for generations. The young, beaten with the "rigor" stick, are being trained to remember old information when our very survival as a nation hinges on their ability to create new information.

Theory T and Theory R have implications for every major issue in education—building design, budgets, classroom furniture arrangements, textbooks, schedules, class size, the role of corporations, the kinds of people attracted to teaching, how kids feel about themselves—everything. Add to that list the newest Big Thing for the New Progressives—"value-added assessment." Theory R tests look nothing like today's machine-scored Theory T tests.

Theory R people, appalled by the current thrust of reform, have been trying for at least six presidential administrations to get Theory T people in Washington to discuss how humans really learn. No luck. So sure are the New Progressives that those who disagree with them are self-serving defenders of the educational status quo, they're unable to see themselves as the true reactionaries.

Sooner or later it will become obvious even to Theory T true believers that their theory only works in a world in which tomorrows are exactly like yesterdays. Unfortunately, when that realization comes, it's unlikely that any teachers who understand Theory R will still be around.

In the above column, I said that "Theory R" teaching was more difficult than "Theory T" teaching. In fact, it's probably more helpful to say that it's just very different. Theory T teachers aren't compelled to listen, but Theory R teachers have no alternative, for dialog is essential. Theory T teachers can file and reuse their presentations, but Theory R teachers have to adapt to the immediate situation, for even the presence or absence of a particular student can change the collective personality of a class. Theory T teachers have no problem handing in their lesson plans for the upcoming week, but Theory R teachers have to fudge or fake, knowing there's no point in forging ahead with a new idea tomorrow if learners haven't yet grasped today's idea. Theory T teachers may even stay on better terms with the custodian, for their classroom chairs are more likely to stay in neat rows and face front, making sweeping the floor easier.

The conceptual scaffold taking gradual shape as instruction proceeds is being constructed by the learner, not the teacher, so the learner sets the pace.

Evaluating Performance

As soon as I suggest to students that what happens in our work together may differ somewhat from what they've come to expect, many immediately jump to what, sadly, is their primary concern. "How do you grade?"

As I've said, years of reinforcement lie behind most students' assumption that "learning" means "remembering." It follows then that at examination time they expect some form of the question, "How much do you remember?" Most don't enjoy the exercise, and they may agree in a discussion that instruction having mere information transfer as its goal is narrow and superficial, but that doesn't mean that they don't (at least initially) prefer examinations of memory over almost everything else. Most do.

I used to try to explore examination and grading theories and philosophies with students, but gave up. I haven't had much success in convincing them (or many teachers, administrators, or education policymakers in state capitols or Washington), that top-down, "rigor" mandates don't work. Infatuation with standardized testing takes education into an intellectual desert. There seems to be no understanding at all of the damage inflicted on the young by the "standards and accountability" fad. Neither is there a willingness to consider that it's significant when delegations of educators from some other countries come to the United States trying to find out why their students, although they may spend far more hours in the study of math and physics than do ours, score no better in tests of scientific reasoning, and generally lag behind in innovation and creativity.

Preoccupied with the race toward the simplistic goals that standardized tests can measure, far more important goals that can't be measured by machine-scored tests are being ignored. The number of correct words per minute a student can type can be counted, but there's no way to precisely determine a student's progress in making more sense of self. Whether or not a student can write a technically correct sentence can be established, but there are no objective measures of the satisfaction that can stem from having fashioned a beautiful phrase. A test can easily be devised to establish that a student knows the names of the planets and their relative distance from the sun. But whether or not instruction has made students more curious about the nature of the universe and the place of humans in it, or helped them recapture the love of learning they had before formal schooling beat it out of them, is an assessment that lies beyond the test maker's skill.

So I keep the comments about evaluation to a minimum, perhaps suggesting merely that my goals for testing aren't much different from those they accept in a mathematics course. On a math exam, one doesn't expect to be asked to do the same problems used in class for illustrative purposes. One is supposed to have learned a process, and the ability to engage in that process is what's being tested.

A Final Word

The fact that I've written an entire book about the general education curriculum doesn't mean that I believe adoption of an acceptable curriculum would cure all the institution's ills. Far from it. I address that problem because it seems to me that what finally matters most in education is what goes on in learners' heads, and that's what the curriculum addresses.

But in the introduction I argued that the insidious process of institutionalization—the tendency of a society's problem-solving procedures to become increasingly dysfunctional—is all but inevitable. This means that every aspect of schooling is subject to the process and should be continuously evaluated and altered as necessary to pursue the institution's aim. I'm not addressing any of those other matters, but my Knight-Ridder/*Tribune* column for May 7, 2005 suggests the kind of wide-ranging change I believe serious education reformers should constantly consider:

Cheap! Maybe that's the key that'll open the door to educational change! The appeal of lower taxes almost always trumps the appeal of higher-quality education, so the trick is to figure out how to educate better with less money...a whole lot less money...so much less money that legislators won't be able to resist removing enough bureaucratic barriers to allow experimentation.

High school reform is on the front burner right now, so let me suggest some ways to save money at that level. Those who think quality lies in doing better what we're already doing will be appalled by the suggestions, but I agree with Joe Graba, former Minnesota Deputy Commissioner of Education: "We can't get the schools we need by improving the schools we have."

So, starting with a clean slate, and thinking "cheap," here's a dozen proposals:

ONE: Take the phrase "neighborhood school" seriously and design around it. Choose local adult-student steering committees to locate, rent or lease centrally located community centers, churches, houses, or other facilities.

TWO: Set maximum school size at 30 to 40 students for morning classes, another 30 to 40 for afternoon or evening classes.

THREE: Hire a three- or four-person teacher team, based on interviews and the team's written program proposal.

FOUR: Right up front, spend whatever is necessary to test and fix sight and hearing problems. It's a waste of money to try to educate kids who're functioning at less than peak potential because they don't hear or see well.

FIVE: Find out who each kid really is. It mystifies me how, with straight faces, we can simultaneously sing the praises of "American individualism" while forcing all kids thru the same narrow program. For a fraction of the cost of present standardized subject-matter tests, every kid's distinctive strengths and weaknesses can be explored using inexpensive, proven inventories of interests, abilities, personalities, and learning styles.

SIX: Eliminate grade levels. Start with where kids are, help them go as far as they're able, and give them a diploma (and perhaps a web site) describing what they've done and can do.

SEVEN: Eliminate textbooks and external tests. They're relics of a bygone era, cost a lot of money, and they're the main support of simplistic ideas about what it means to teach and learn.

EIGHT: Stop chopping knowledge up into "subjects." Knowledge is seamless, and the brain processes it most efficiently when it's integrated.

NINE: Push responsibility for teaching specific skills and knowledge on to users of those skills and knowledge—employers. Specialized, occupation-related instruction such as that now being offered in magnet schools will never be able to keep up with either the variety or the rate of change. Employers will resist, so sweeten the pot with subsidies as necessary. (A bonus: Apprenticeship and intern arrangements will go a long way toward smoothing the transition into responsible adulthood.)

TEN: Eliminate school buses, food services, athletic departments, athletic fields, cops on campus, non-teaching administrators, attendance officers, extra-curricular activities. (And add into the tax savings much of the estimated $50,000-plus it costs each year to keep poorly educated kids locked up in prisons.)

ELEVEN: Strip away all the non-academic roles and responsibilities state legislators piled on schools during the 20th century. Create independent municipal support systems for neighborhood-level, multi-age programs for art, dance, drama, sports, and anything else "extra-curricular" for which a local need or interest is apparent.

TWELVE: Drastically shrink central administrations. Have them coordinate the forming of teacher teams, and relieve those teams of paper shuffling, resource acquisition, and other non-instructional tasks.

School doesn't need to take all day every day. Suggestions FIVE thru NINE will make it possible to accomplish more in three hours than is now being accomplished in six. The special-interest, personal learning project which every student should always have underway can be done on her and his own time.

Not incidentally, I'm concerned with matters in addition to functional schools—the creation of a sense of neighborhood and community, the expansion of community service activities, and vastly increased contact between generations. Cutting out all the non-academic responsibilities will open up time for all kinds of fascinating, new, growth-producing activity.

Don't like my proposal? Dream up your own. But keep another Joe Graba insight in mind: "Everybody wants the schools to be better; but almost nobody wants them to be different."

APPENDIX

In *What's Worth Learning?*, I've argued that traditional schooling barely scratches the surface of learner potential, and that performance remains basically flat despite nonstop reform initiatives because of our deeply flawed nineteenth century curriculum.

No matter first-rate teachers, the latest technology, enlightened administrators, generous budgets, supportive parents, highly motivated learners, the harnessing of market forces, or any other currently popular cure for what ails education, if the curriculum is poor, the education will be poor.

Major improvement in intellectual performance is possible, but it won't come from doing longer and harder what we've always done. The skills and knowledge learners most need but aren't getting are those that help them *cope* with information—helps them understand the "mechanics" of the mental processes they use to select, organize, evaluate, relate, synthesize, and make practical use of information.

The appendix to *What's Worth Learning?* titled, "Connections: Investigating Reality," helps learners learn how they learn. In a manner consistent with General Systems Theory, and reflecting recent insights into how the brain processes information, it weaves together content and process to create a comprehensive, supradisciplinary general education course of study for adolescents and older students.

The program's extensive use of firsthand learner experience makes conceptual concreteness, relevance, rigor, complex thought, and intrinsic motivation, inherent.

"Connections" should be seen as just a start—a rough first draft of a "comprehensive scope and sequence" (education-speak for what to teach, in what order). For this reason, instead of the Appendix appearing here, it's on the Internet, is of course free, needing merely to be downloaded.

This unorthodox arrangement has many advantages, chief among them being the ease with which "Connections: Investigating Reality" can be elaborated and updated in response to social change, to new research, and to the insights of those of differing ethnic and cultural backgrounds. The course is accompanied by a parallel online tool encouraging users to comment, suggest improvements or alternatives to activities, and propose adaptations for particular learner populations. It's hoped that instructional activities, even ones that could be completed in a day or two, will prompt users to expand and reinforce ideas of their own design before moving on to the next activity.

In writing "Connections," a determined effort was made to walk a narrow line between providing enough support to give users confidence about the way ahead, but not so much that it gets in the way of the experience, expertise, and creativity they bring to the program.

A word of warning to administrators and policymakers. Those who see merit in "Connections: Investigating Reality" should avoid any temptation to impose the program "top-down." Calling attention to the program, granting permission to consider its use, exploring its potential, encouraging dialog, and supporting experimentation, are administrative actions most likely to yield understanding and success.

"Connections" was written with all adolescents in mind. However, given the current infatuation with standardized test scores, educators most likely to be interested in it are those working with learners either so far ahead or so far behind their peers their test scores are of little concern to decision makers.

To access the Appendix, "Connections: Investigating Reality," please visit the following URLs:

- http://www.marionbrady.com/2008/10/investigating-systems-course-of-study.html

or

- http://infoagepub.com/brady-worth

ABOUT THE AUTHOR

Marion Brady began his career in education in 1952, teaching English, social studies, and other classes in a small, semirural high school in northeastern Ohio. In the years following, he taught at every level from sixth grade through university, was a teacher educator, county-level school administrator, and consultant to publishers, states, and foundations. He has authored textbooks and professional books, contributed many articles and commentaries to domestic and foreign journals, was for 7 years an education columnist for Knight-Ridder/Tribune Information Services, is an invited guest blogger for the *Washington Post* and Truthout.org, and a visitor and observer of schools across America and abroad.

INDEX